Aging in Place
Conversations

Aging in Place Conversations: What Industry Experts Have to Say

National Aging in Place Council
Contributing Authors

Tara Ballman

Bonnie Dobbs

Scott Fulton

Mary Kay Furiasse

Ronnie Genser

C. Vicki Gold

Fritzi Gros-Daillon

Sue Haviland

Peter Klamkin

Gina Knight

Ryan McEniff

Andriana Mendez

Amy Miller

Wayne Mitchell

Courtney Nalty

Deanne O'Rear Cameron

Carmen Perry-Tevaga

Julianne Rizzo

Steve Toll

Julia Uhll

Jawbone Publishing   California   2022

Printed in the United States of America.

The content of *Aging in Place Conversations: What Industry Experts Have to Say* is for informational purposes only. It is not advice or guarantee of outcome. Information written, gathered, shared, and presented by the authors is their opinion and other resources provided are of reputable origination. The National Aging in Place Council and the authors are not responsible for errors or omissions in reporting or explanation. No individuals or industry professionals should use the information, resources, or tools contained herein for the purposes of self-diagnosis, self-treatment of any health-related condition or for financial or legal advice and strategies contained in this book without first consulting with your own healthcare professional, financial advisor, tax professional or conducting your own research and due diligence. The National Aging in Place Council and the authors of this book give no assurance or warranty regarding the accuracy, timeliness, or applicability of the content.

Library of Congress Cataloging-in-Publication Data Control Number:
Name: National Aging in Place Council
Title: Aging in Place Conversations: What Industry Experts Have to Say
Description: California, Jawbone Publishing, 2022 | Includes bibliographical references.
Identifiers: ISBN: 978-1-59094-260-4
Subjects: Aging Parents, Aging, Eldercare, Aging in Place
Book cover design by Jake Donnelly

Praise for
Aging in Place Conversations

"Today's retirees are radically rethinking their new purpose, freedoms and challenges, and the changing role of their home and community. Aging in Place Conversations: What Industry Experts Have to Say provides readers rare insights into the important role of 'place' and how to take early action to make the most of life's third age."

- Ken Dychtwald, PhD, CEO, Age Wave, coauthor of
Age Wave and What Retirees Want:
A Holistic View of Life's Third Age

"This is the must-have companion (guide) for individuals and designers alike to inspire connection and safety, with aesthetically beautiful home planning, to support all stages in the second half of life."

- Mary Jo Saavedra Gerontologist, CMC, CAPS, CSA, SD
Author of *Eldercare 101: A Practical Guide to*
Later Life Planning, Care, and Wellbeing

"When you begin to see all these factors, the idea that you would know what is available and how to engage it as a consumer, novice to these particular circumstances, is a joke. That is where the help these authors offer becomes so critical. And what do they all recommend? Planning."

- Louis Tenenbaum, Founder,
HomesRenewed Coalition

"Informed and aware, Aging in Place is filled with opportunities to extend health, happiness, and independence. This rare collection of subject matter experts opens the door into knowledge few will think to ask, until a moment of crisis. Opportunities await those who take this knowledge forward with meaningful, early actions."

— **Scott Fulton, Chair,**
National Aging in Place Council

"Aging in Place Conversations is an essential resource for new and existing retirees as well as professionals. The experts within the National Aging in Place Council are leading the way to healthier, happy, and more connected lifestyles by helping people avoid common misconceptions and pitfalls, while taking advantage of new trends and technology."

— **Robert Laura, Founder,**
Retirement Coaches Association

"The most successful Aging in Place plans are created before a crisis occurs. The expert information provided in this book will help you understand your options, the cost of those options, and how to access available resources - regardless of your income level. Start your plan today!"

— **Tara Ballman, MBA, Executive Director,**
National Aging in Place Council

Contents

Foreword

This book is clearly a labor of love and passion.

The group that wrote these chapters joined forces to do so because they care so deeply about their subject. Their subject is their clients. Their subject is you. Such wisdom, caring and guidance is not easy to come by. On the occasion when you see it, it behooves you to listen, to pay attention and to follow their advice. How can you turn away from that sort of gift?

The book uses common questions to paint a comprehensive picture of the issues we face in our aging experiences. Of course, everyone's lived experience is different, but by drawing attention to the common issues and possible solutions, the painting becomes a roadmap of the preparation and readiness likely to ease your experience as it plays out. A few words came to mind as I read through the chapters and issues:

- Passion
- Commitment
- Complex
- Dynamic
- Planning

I've already mentioned passion. These writers, from a field as diverse as the topics and issues they discuss, all have personal experience that led them to be offering this advice. Whether that experience is a neighbor or loved one whose aging experience was sub-optimal, or one they were able to help successfully, it changed their lives. They decided this topic was too important and their potential role was so rewarding that they pivoted their careers to this focus. That is a lot of commitment. It indicates the degree their caring informs their work. We readers are the beneficiaries.

Aging in place is about the interplay of your home, finances, and community with changing health. There are a lot of factors. All houses are different, and the way we use and occupy them are even more different. The same is true for finances. Each of us has priorities about how and for what we will use our available money. Each of us is part of many communities ranging from close ones of family and neighbors, to the societal level of government agencies, businesses, and not-for-profit services. You may be only barely aware of some of these communities and a regular user or participant in others, but this book helps guide us to engage the unique blend of possible activity, advice, assistance, proximity, and eligibility that meets our needs and desires. Once health and associated health expenses color this resource matrix the complexity can become overwhelming and the guidance even more critical.

Aging is always dynamic. Everyone's health is dynamic. You feel fine, get a cold...or worse.... And hopefully with rest or treatment you get better. Aging intensifies this cycle significantly. Each health incident takes longer for recovery. From some there is never full recovery. It all comes at a rush and the "health system" has processes, schedules and rules that are opaque to "consumers." Once we are in a health incident all timing, expectations, and experience other than "let's see what happens" are out the window. Scrambling through unknown passages is the unfortunate norm.

When you begin to see all of these factors, the idea that you would know what is available and how to engage it as a consumer, novice to these particular circumstances, is a joke. That is where the help these authors offer becomes so critical. And what do they all recommend? Planning.

But planning is not typical. Behavioral economics research shows that we have trouble imagining ourselves in circumstances we have not experienced. Research shows that, though we recognize that the last ten years has not turned out as we might have expected, we somehow believe the next ten will turn out as we picture them. Human nature. We can't fight it but, with thoughtful, attentive preparation, we can ease the odds of things going badly. So, you might consider the wisdom in this book to be a bettor's "tip" like which horse has a better chance or which football player has a sore ankle. Planning for aging in place is your chance to play the odds.

Another finger on the scale is motivation. In recent years behavior change techniques have become science. Nudges are the coin of the realm. By studying what has worked in similar situations we can design 'nudges' that have a good chance of influencing people to act.

Around 2015 I found myself impressed at the way growing hybrid and electric car markets and solar collector installations followed tax incentive nudges. These policies were collective planning tools that shifted individual spending to shared goals that use less carbon, and slow climate change. Could planning for aging in place be viewed through a similar lens? Can policy encourage individual purchases that ease the odds of ending up in a crisis situation in which we feel out of control?

I gathered the forces of the HomesRenewed™ Coalition to push for tax incentives that will influence homeowners to make their homes safer and more accessible. These updates, making homes safer and more accessible (many described in the pages to follow), will reduce costly and life-changing falls, reduce the hours of caregiving needed and shorten rehab stays...all reducing misery, discomfort and the health costs born by Medicare, Medicaid, and our individual accounts.

I finish with two requests for action. Please take heed of the wisdom offered in this book. Begin the planning that will ease your own aging experience and the collective impact of our aging population on our society. The home is a linchpin to the potential for successful aging in place. Play the odds by installing accessibility updates to your home and encouraging others. Second, join the movement for tax incentives in order to make the updating of homes and attention to aging in place even more commonplace.

Take action. We all benefit.

- **Louis Tenenbaum**

Named one of Next Avenue's "Influencers in Aging" in 2016, Louis Tenenbaum is a leading authority on aging in place. He writes and speaks extensively on the importance of a safe and accessible home. He was one of the first contractors to focus his remodeling business on aging in place. He saw that, although there is a great need for properly updated housing, few people are focusing on the house, the physical structure, itself. Instead, industry, government and consumers are interested in sexier issues, such as new tech and hospital at home. But if you can't get into your house or use your bathroom, you can't benefit from these services.

In addition to recognition from Next Avenue, Louis won a HIVE (Housing, Innovation, Vision and Economics) award from the building industry. Uniquely straddling the building, aging and policy worlds, his mission is to make American homes safe for older people by educating and advocating for change.

Louis is now leading HomesRenewed™ Coalition, the driving force behind the bipartisan Home Modifications for Accessibility Act, HR 7676, that will incentivize homeowners to make their homes safer and more accessible. For more information, visit https://www.homesrenewedcoalition.com/

A Certified Aging in Place Specialist, Louis has been remodeling homes and consulting on accessibility for decades. A graduate of the University of Michigan, Louis has two grown children and lives in Montgomery County, Maryland.

Acknowledgements

First, we would like to thank our author team for devoting their time, energy, and expertise for making this book possible. Because of their combined experience, ideas, and commitment to help older adults and their families, our communities can work together to offer solutions to successfully create a plan for aging in place. Our gratitude is extended to the following author contributors:

Tara Ballman, MBA
Bonnie Dobbs
Scott Fulton
Mary Kay Furiasse, BSN, JD, LLM
Ronnie Genser
C. Vicki Gold, PT, MA
Fritzi Gros-Daillon, MS, CSA, CAPS, UDCP, SHSS
Sue Haviland
Peter Klamkin
Gina Knight
Ryan McEniff
Andriana Mendez
Amy Miller
Wayne Mitchell
Courtney Nalty
Deanne O'Rear Cameron
Carmen Perry-Tevaga
Julianne Rizzo, RN, MBA, CSA
Steve Toll, BS, QDCS
Julia Uhll

There are other participants in this worthwhile book project who we want to acknowledge; without them, this book never could have happened. We want to extend our appreciation to Tricia Bell, who worked behind the scenes coordinating nationwide Zoom calls, email communications, and a dozen other activities that ensured a smooth book production from start to finish. As for our beautiful book cover, we thankfully acknowledge the artistic talents of Jake Donnelly. Many thanks to Swanee Ballman who served as editor to review the manuscript so we could take it to the next step - publication. And of course, Melissa Newton of Millcreek Media Group, who managed our team of authors beautifully!

And now for the main reason we wrote this book: you. Whether you are an older adult, family member, caregiver, service provider, advocate of an older adult, or a product developer or service provider for the senior market, this book is for you. By working together as a community, sharing our knowledge, experiences, ideas, and commitment, we can promise positive outcomes to those who are entering the phase of life that should be a time of safety, engagement, and choices.

We encourage you to share this book with family, friends, colleagues, and leaders in your community. Together, we can make a difference and the dream of aging in place a reality.

The National Aging in Place Council
www.AgeinPlace.org

How to Use This Book

The mission of the National Aging in Place Council (NAIPC) is "to bring professionals and communities together to champion Aging in Place through collaboration and education." Our members work with older adults to provide information, products, services, and resources that allows individuals to remain in the residence of their choosing for as long as possible while remaining safe, secure, and engaged in life.

How do you ensure you remain independent and safe in the home of your choosing? By creating a plan that will prepare you for any situation should the unexpected occur and challenge your ability to live independently. You can make better choices *now* for a smoother transition into your latter years so they can be more fully enjoyed, comfortable, and engaged.

A benefit of working with NAIPC is that you have access to a diverse group of experts. When considering the best way to combine this collective knowledge of seasoned professionals for our first book, we decided a question-and-answer format for *Aging in Place Conversations: What Industry Experts Have to Say* would be the best approach. After all, when we are researching and seeking solutions to a problem, it begins with asking questions.

Following "What Does Aging in Place Mean?" and "The Five Pillars of Aging," the remaining chapters will follow the NAIPC's Five Pillars, which are the core principles of crafting an aging in place plan. These Five Pillars are: Housing, Health and Wellness, Personal Finance, Transportation, and Community and Social Interaction. Each chapter presents common questions and scenarios that older adults and their families may encounter in their aging-in-place research. Some questions have multiple author responses, but each author brings their unique experiences, stories, or insights to the subject. (Each author is listed in the Biographical Index of Contributing Authors at the end of this book.)

We have incorporated QR codes, a technology-based tool for convenient quick-access to additional information, throughout the book.

What is a QR code? QR stands for "Quick Response" and the code stores data in the form of a barcode. When the barcode is scanned with a mobile phone camera or app, you are sent to a mobile-friendly website.

Point your smartphone at the QR code below to go to the NAIPC's main website: www.ageinplace.org

Wherever you see a QR code in this book, we invite you to use your smartphone to connect to a website with additional resources. The full website link is included as well should you opt to look up a resource on your computer.

Need more help understanding QR codes? Watch this quick video from AARP's Online Learning Videos at https://www.youtube.com/watch?v=8KHHFquutS8 or scan here:

We invite you to learn from our authors here, and encourage you to engage and learn from the professionals in your community.

We only have one chance to get it right, and if there was ever a time to commit to excellence, this is it. Open the door to age into new and enlightening opportunities by making your place, a home that far surpasses your current needs, in a community filled with companionship and support. With that in mind, as you proceed through this book, take notes, formulate a plan, and start making it your own by accessing the best resources that can support your dreams.

Need a place to start? Complete our online "My Needs Summary" at https://ageinplace.org/myneeds/ or scan the QR code here:

To download your own copy of the 24-page *Act III: Your Plan for Aging in Place* template, scan here:

1
What Does Aging in Place Mean?
Scott Fulton

"Other than a few wrinkles and some grey hairs, I still feel as young as ever." It's familiar self-talk, and it's a good thing to feel positive and energetic. After all, aging well is one of the most precious gifts that life can offer. Embrace it, and aging in every "place" we find ourselves is filled with appealing opportunities and ever-renewing perspectives on life. Deny it, and it has a nasty habit of blindsiding us, stealing years from living well and years from life itself.

Aging into the twenty-first century will be unlike anything experienced in human history. Fantastic opportunities await the well prepared, those committed to preserving the dignity and independence for themselves and those they love. Sadly, many less prepared will be swept up by the perfect storm that is just beginning to brew, bringing unprecedented challenges and unchartered waters. Your timing to pick up this book could not be better.

The twentieth century saw a western construct emerge that devalued elders and a conscious mindset of denying our own aging. That construct also caused us to put off age-related plans at the same time life expectancy was quickly rising. Harmless enough in the short term, but time has a habit of slipping away, until one single event triggers a tsunami of age-related housing, medical, emotional, transportation, financial, and family issues that overwhelm our best intentions and ability to cope. The trigger might be a doctor's diagnosis, the passing of a life partner, or one of several common earthshattering life events. In an instant, everything in our world is turned upside down. Suddenly, hundreds of urgent and important decisions we never envisioned are thrust, not just in our lap, but in our loved ones' laps as well. Those who serve older adults see this play out every day, hearing the familiar phrases: "I wish ..., If only ..., I meant to..."

Best Before Date

The act of retirement is thought to be static, so what could there possibly be to plan for? We forget that every tangible thing in life comes with a "Best Before Date," and that includes our homes. Thankfully, we can extend the livability lifespan of our homes with some key upgrades, but those come with a caveat. The best options are the ones we have today. Things that make living enjoyable and rewarding get harder with time, unless we actively plan for ways to keep them fun and easy longer, by extending their Best Before Date. Otherwise, the best options naturally expire, and we're left with the least appealing offerings, usually paying a premium for them, and getting less. Ouch! Every option can be put off. But with deferral comes missed opportunities to enjoy a sustainable lifestyle, better health, and lower long-term living costs.

If aging in place evokes images of institutional settings, and a life centered around metal ramps and bedpans, it's little surprise that planning has remained on the backburner. A perception that all options are unappealing inevitably leads to deferral, not action. Confounding this is a false sense of awareness of the complex physical and technological aspects of older adult housing.

Imagine the reaction of a sweet couple, having lived in a house that helped raise their family and served them well for forty years, being told that their home is deficient and will not support the retirement plans they've clung to for decades. It conflicts directly with forty years of trusted evidence. Their denial and anger are understandable, and they hastily usher the bearer of bad news out the door.

It's only after a trigger event, when everything is on the line, that they'll make their way through the stages of grieving their old home and find their way to acceptance. Acceptance, however, can often mean they are forced out of the one sure thing they had counted on for decades, because they hadn't taken appropriate actions when they had the opportunity. If that weren't bad enough, they quickly discover that all the preferred living options they thought were available, have all vanished. They have Best Before Dates, too.

Thrust into the role of primary caregiver, spouses and adult children are suddenly overwhelmed by simple daily chores like cooking, cleaning, shopping, and gardening. No one mentioned that caregiving was one of the hardest jobs on the planet, especially in a home environment never intended for older adults. When health deals a heavy blow, every ounce of energy is consumed in trying to keep things afloat, in a life-raft seemingly filled with holes. No amount of help seems to be enough, and families become stressed beyond measure.

Aging in Place College

What if we approached aging in place like it was a college degree? What if we did our homework, invested time each day discovering the best possibilities, and learned more about housing, health, finance, transportation, and social connection, like it truly mattered? Would a world of opportunities open up for us, just as it did in our education experiences decades earlier? You bet it would. Those who roll up their sleeves, and do the real work, discover there are a lot of gaps in their early thinking, but they fix them and focus on the opportunities. They don't get it perfect, but they cover the key bases and protect their families from having to make big decisions amid a major crisis. It frees them to pursue their dream to go back to college, teach in their community, attend a great-grandchild's graduation, and maybe even host their 100th birthday party in their own home.

Aging into the twenty-first century means you can prepare to thrive. We've all got some homework in front of us. I encourage you to look to the opportunities that will be challenging, and that offer deep fulfillment and sense of purpose - the "why" behind our choices.

Learn from the Pros

Wisdom in aging resides in the professionals who work in the field every day - the authors gathered here in this unprecedented book project. These are the people who navigate families through a vast array of situations you and I could never predict. This is their world, and this is your window to learn from the wisdom they have acquired from the thousands of older adults they've been privileged to serve.

Whether you're just starting your retirement journey, the child of a widow, or a seasoned lifelong learner, this book will speak to you on both practical and emotional levels. As you read the answers to many top questions, remember that successful aging in place relies on strong interdependence. The independence we all aspire to will rely on a strong foundation of meaningful physical and emotional relationships, more than at any time in our lives.

2
The Five Pillars of Aging
Tara Ballman, Julia Uhll

To create a strong foundation for an Aging in Place plan, it is important to consider all Five Pillars of Aging. These Five Pillars were identified by NAIPC over fifteen years ago and serve as discussion points for older adults, families, and others in this community who make aging in place achievable.

To provide you a better understanding of how to apply the Five Pillars to your life as you review the questions in this book, let's first talk about the Five Pillars and why they matter.

What Are the Five Pillars of Aging?
The Five Pillars consist of the following:
1) Housing
2) Health and Wellness
3) Personal Finance
4) Transportation
5) Community and Social Interaction

These Five Pillars are the critical points that will influence, for good or bad, our overall life as we age. Each pillar impacts the others. The decisions you make about different aspects of your personal finances, whether it be Medicare or a reverse mortgage, impacts the balance in your checking account, which affects your housing options. How you establish your housing arrangement will play a role in your transportation and your socialization. Each pillar is interconnected.

The reality is we have to pay attention to the finer details of the Five Pillars in our aging journey. Why? When we are proactive in making choices about what we want our life to look like inside those pillars, we can hope for better outcomes. If we want our aging experience to be a positive one, you must start making your plans now. The good news is that after you have read *Aging in Place Conversations: What Industry Experts Have to Say*, you will have a clearer understanding of how the Five Pillars play such an important part of your aging journey. Plus, the content you gather from these pages will give you the information you need to make the best decisions for your age in place plan.

Here is some more good news; it is never too late to begin making your own customized aging in place plan. Of course, reading this book is a great first step in addressing the essential pillars so you can sustain a safe and secure lifestyle in your home. As you read through the questions and answers provided by our fellow expert authors, we highly recommend you do so in tandem with a free 24-page planning template called *Act III: Your Plan for Aging in Place.* To download your own copy of the template, scan the QR code below or visit https://naipc.memberclicks.net.

If you need assistance getting started, complete the "My Needs Summary" at https://ageinplace.org/myneeds/ or scan the QR code here:

What is *Act III: Your Plan for Aging in Place* ?

The NAIPC developed this template to be a guide for older adults and their families to develop a plan for aging in place. These results provide an overview of the areas within the Five Pillars that may need work based on your responses. Here is the exciting part. If you live near a local NAIPC chapter, a member of the chapter can review your "My Needs Summary" with you. If a chapter is not in your area, not a problem; a NAIPC National staff member can help you.

Your Aging in Place Plan Starts Today

Learning about the Five Pillars of Aging can offer older adults a powerful resource to take control of their aging in place lifestyle. Ultimately, it offers the freedom of choice to make the latter decades of living filled with security, support, and comfort.

Pillar 1: Housing

When we think about the word "housing" as we age, many different concepts to home living may come to mind. It can be transitioning to an assisted living space. Perhaps it means downsizing or moving to a warmer climate where snow is something you only see on the Weather Channel. For an increasing number of older adults, "housing" means remaining in their current home as they age. Regardless of the current location called "home," they are all aging in place.

A recent AARP *Home and Community Preferences Survey* revealed that 77 percent of adults age fifty and older wanted to remain in their homes for the long term. That statistic has remained consistent for over ten years. Establishing a safe and comfortable home to maintain valued independence is on the top of the list when creating your age in place plan.

We have provided some key questions and several scenarios to serve as a backdrop for situations that are common for older adults on the issue of housing. Whether it is to know what actions need to be taken following a loved one's hospital stay or how to initiate a conversation with your family about aging in place, we think this is a good place to start your plan.

Question 1: *I hear different opinions on housing as people age. It makes it very confusing. Some recommend moving to an assisted living community while others are moving to be closer to their families. I would like to remain in my home, but I need to understand my options.*

Julianne Rizzo, RN, MBA, CSA:

Aging in place is vastly different for individuals. Sometimes it is no longer safe for someone to live on their own, some might be lonely and in need of socialization or may desire a simpler maintenance free lifestyle. Below is a brief outline the different types of senior living options for older adults.

Independent Living

Independent living is designed exclusively for older adults. It is exactly what the words states - independent. This type of living is attractive to older adults who are interested in downsizing their large homes or for empty nesters. Also, it is a good option for people looking to enjoy maintenance-free living. No more yard work, roof repairs, or flooded basements to worry about. You can come and go as you please, you can partake in as many activities you like, but you are independent.

Residences come in all shapes and sizes: studios, one-bedroom, two-bedrooms, or private cottages. Some have a full kitchen, and others have kitchenettes (no stove/ovens). They offer meal plans, so you do not need to cook anymore. They offer services like housekeeping, planned outings, laundry service, and local transportation for a fee.

Assisted Living

Assisted living communities are designed for those older adults who require assistance with two or three activities of daily living (ADLs): feeding yourself, getting dressed, transferring in and out of a sitting position, toileting, and personal hygiene care.

Assisted living offers private or shared rooms (may live with a spouse or a companion to keep costs down), they are considered apartment style living. They come in studio, one-bedroom, and two-bedrooms. They include all the same benefits of living in an independent living community (housekeeping, planned outings, laundry service, and local transportation), but are included in monthly rent. One extra service that is offered with assisted living is medication management.

This type of living option offers 24/7 nursing care with regular check-ins to make sure the older adult is safe. Most will provide the older adult with a medical alert pendent and pull cords in the room to alert staff if help is needed.

The federal government does not regulate assisted living communities, which falls on individual states to license communities and perform regular visits to ensure compliance.

Memory Care

Memory Care Communities specialize in caring for people suffering from some form of Dementia. There are over three hundred different types of Dementia, however the four most common are:

• Alzheimer's disease
• Vascular dementia
• Lewy body dementia
• Frontotemporal dementia

These types of communities are secured units to ensure safety, since people with this disease tend to wander and get lost. Because it is a locked unit, every resident must have a clinical diagnosis of Dementia from a physician or neuropsychologist. The staff is provided with specialized training to care for people with Dementia because residents exhibit challenging behaviors due to cognitive and memory impairment.

This type of community can aid with all ADLs and offer 24/7 supervision. They typically have safeguards in place to ensure safety of the residents, such as door alarms and cameras in the rooms. Programming is key to keeping the residents engaged and on a regular schedule.

This type of senior living offers mostly studios and/or companion rooms with just enough space for a bed, nightstand, chair, and bathroom. This unit is either a stand-alone building, or a separate wing of an assisted living community.

I hope I have explained the different types of senior living options where older adults can age in place, whatever that looks like for you. We are living longer and stronger and there are many different options for older adults to *live*!

Amy Miller:

For those who want to remain in their homes and receive care from family members, I recommend writing a family caregiving agreement in advance. A family caregiving agreement allows loved ones to take on the daily chores and caregiving for a predetermined payment. Adult children and grandchildren may take a leave of absence or quit their jobs to be available, which comes at the loss of income, benefits, and retirement savings. Family members who live far away, busy with their own families and work, or estranged are unaware of the emotional and financial impact caused by caregiving. When I talk with my clients, the dad is often appreciative when their sons or grandsons step up to assist with lifting and personal care such as shaving.

Keep a record of all care provided. The record of care includes the date, time, activity and who completed the task. Family members then know when activities are completed, and the record can be used to invoice caregivers. It also provides protection for you if your bank asks about large payment transactions (to combat financial exploitation), or you are looking to qualify for elderly waiver or medical assistance programs under Medicare per the five-year look back period.

As a respite for caregivers and a means to provide engaging activities with peers, older adults look forward to attending a local adult care program. Most cities will have a local senior center for older community members who want to meet and make new friends, attend exercise classes, play cards and backgammon, work on their tech skills, do arts and crafts, or attend speaker series. Many programs offer day trips to local sites and historical landmarks. To find a community program near you, visit some of the links provided in the "Notes and Additional Resources" chapter at the end of this book.

One program I found in my local community was a Montessori adult and child care program that offers a unique, home-like setting for those who attended. While the children and older adults have their own space, they come together for story time and sing-a-longs. Often the grandparents will be found in the infant rooms rocking a child to sleep or folding laundry to assist the staff. Doing these daily tasks has been found to be especially helpful for those living with dementia. Meals are prepared by a professional chef. These programs are designed to have older adults live like they would at home but with professional supervision.

Families ask me whether they need to pay this out-of-pocket or use insurance to cover the cost for family caregivers and adult day programs. Adult day centers are popular due to their affordability and variety of events. The costs can range from $25 to $75 a day. Half-day options can be arranged based on the needs of the caregivers and families. Most families pay for adult day care out of pocket. Medicare, Medicaid, and Veteran's benefits may provide funding for those who meet income requirements through county or state funded grants and programs.

Long-term care insurance may pay the family member if they have been certified as a personal care assistant, and it is set up in advance. Rates paid by insurance may differ from state to state. To find the rate you might be paid, visit the Family Caregiver Alliance website at www.caregiver.org or scan the QR code below:

Loans may be taken out tax free from a whole life insurance policy to cover these expenses. Medicare will pay family members for those who meet income qualifications and other requirements and training. Some families agree to have one of the family members pay for their parents' expenses. Do not forget that you can pay $16,000 to your caregiver tax free under the gifting guidelines in the IRS code. To make sure this meets tribal, state, and local guidelines, consult with an attorney, financial planner, or tax professional.

Andriana Mendez:

Whether you decide to age in place or move, how do you go about downsizing what you own? Your children may not wish to keep your possessions. How do you go about letting them know how important these things are to you as part of your family history?

While a home often comes with a sense of pride and comfort, your relationship with it can change over time. Events or lifestyles may have you considering if "home" could be simpler, smaller, or more accessible. Deciding to downsize to a more manageable space may even give you the opportunity for a new start.

Conversely, you may have decided that you would like to stay put. However, maybe you are frustrated with clutter or disorganization, or have been painfully avoiding certain areas throughout your home. Perhaps you worry that you or your partner may trip and fall on things that do not have a proper place.

Regardless of downsizing or aging in place, you will want to approach the situation with a similar mindset: your things should make you happy and should tell the story of who you are. Anything else does not belong in your home.

How to Start Sorting

Allow yourself the time and space to emotionally process it all. You will be deciding what to give away, donate, discard, or take with you if you've moving. This is a chance for you to really ask yourself what things still serve your lifestyle now and what will represent your future legacy. A lifetime of items can't just be packed up and moved out in one day. What is important, though, is that you put one foot in front of another and start the process.

As you do this, a wonderful form of healing and processing takes place - the act of telling stories that are associated with your items, even if you choose not to keep them. Our clients find that simply relating their stories gives them the closure they need. Many have never been asked, or given the opportunity to verbally express, what something represents to them. Alternatively, you can take photos of your items and make a scrapbook or write a short story to accompany the photo of the item or use an app like Artifcts.com.

Helpful Tips

Start with your goal: (1) downsize and move, or (2) declutter and organize. Then, create a layout plan and/or a checklist with simple tasks at the top followed by more complex tasks. Choose a time of day or the week that is manageable for you and consider if you need an accountability buddy to help you stay on track. If you like to work alone, find some nice music that fits how you are feeling that day. Set the timer. Don't overdo it. Try to pave a steady path of moving forward.

As you sort through your things, ask yourself:
- Have I used this in the last six months?
- Does it work?
- Do I have another object that performs the same function?
- Does this item support my current lifestyle?
- Do I personally have an attachment to this item?
- Does this item still mean something to me?
- Will this item continue to tell my life story after I am gone?

If you find that this task is still overwhelming or need a neutral person to assist, a Certified Senior Move Manager can help. Many of us are available, and we have made it our mission to support you through this process. We provide a plan, compassionate guidance, and the experience to know the safest and most effective way to help you downsize or declutter for a more empowered life. To find professionals near you, visit the National Association of Senior Move Managers at www.nasmm.org/find-a-move-manager or scan the QR code below:

Courtney Nalty:

Various questions should be considered when determining if moving to a senior living community is the best option for you.

If I choose to move to a senior living community, can I take my pet?

When moving into a senior community, the ability to bring one's pet/s is dependent on the level of care (living) that someone will need. Most Active Adult Apartments and Communities as well as Independent Living Communities will usually allow one pet. However, it can come with some caveats, such as the type of pet, size of the pet, additional fees, etc. Most communities will have a "resident agreement" or lease document that can explain their pet policy.

As for Assisted Living or Nursing Care, most of these types of communities will not allow pets because the staff ends up not only caring for the resident/patient, but also the pet. This takes away from the quality of care and time from others needing assistance in the community.

There may be exceptions to the pet rules, such as a person moving into Assisted Living or Nursing Facility for minimal reasons (i.e., diabetes management, transportation needs, meal preparation, housekeeping assistance, etc.) or if the pet is a service dog.

An idea for those moving into a community that does not allow pets is to have a family member, neighbor, or good friend adopt their pet and bring them to visit as often as possible. The older adult could offer to continue to pay for vet fees and food.

Can my adult child go with me?

As with bringing a pet, having your adult child move into a community with you will depend on a few things:

1. Age of the adult child. Most communities will welcome those over age fifty-five. Depending on the by-laws or rules of the community/organization (e.g., if it is a non-profit), a certain percentage of residents can be under age fifty-five (about 15-20 percent), but ask specifically at each place you are considering.

2. Needs of the adult child. If the child has special needs, whether it is physical or mental, many communities will welcome them. However, the adult child must meet all the medical and financial requirements. For instance, if an adult child is fifty years old and suffers from a mental illness, they must provide all medical, legal, and financial records. If the older parent dies before the adult child, proof of financial stability to maintain residency will be necessary. Otherwise, a plan will need to be put in place for a possible move.

Please note that each community has different rules and regulations. It is imperative you specifically ask the above questions at the beginning of your research.

How long does it take to sell my home and then move into a new living community?

The answer to the above question depends on where you currently live and where you are moving. First, do your research in finding the right community for you or the older adult you are assisting. Once you have selected a place to live, find out on availability, wait-list, and timeline. From that point you can begin researching real estate agents, moving companies, senior moving managers (or senior relocation specialists), and estate liquidators.

If the sale looks to be taking longer than expected, there are ways to pay for the initial fees and dues. Below are some options to consider:

- Reverse mortgage
- Home Equity line of credit
- Sell directly to a company that specializes in purchasing housing from seniors (senior transition specialist)
- Liquidate any investments (art, vehicles, mutual funds, stocks, bonds, life insurance, IRAs, etc.)

It is important to meet with your financial advisor, accountant, or banker to discuss your options. If you are waiting for an opening in a community, start decluttering your home at your own pace. You can get assistance from family and friends or hire a company that specializes in cleaning, organizing, and decluttering.

Question 2: *My spouse is coming home from the hospital and prefers to heal comfortably at home. He will be in a wheelchair for a few months, maybe longer. Our home is not wheelchair accessible. Can he stay at home? Who do I call to get help? Can any services be provided in at home to help me? What home modifications do I need?*

Gina Knight:

All seniors and their families have different modifications based on their living arrangements and medical needs. Most homes and apartments can adapt to temporary or permanent modifications. However, many times older adults have ongoing conditions where relocation is a better long-term option.

All older adults are highly recommended to initially begin with a comprehensive Age in Place assessment from a Certified Aging in Place Specialist providing a personalized in-home evaluation plan for the home. Below are modifications to that should be considered:

1. Home Entrance

All modifications, regardless of the long-term solution, start with the home's entrance. Depending on the elevation height of the porch area, you may consider an exterior wheelchair lift or a wheelchair ramp (metal or wood) for a safe entrance. Keep in mind, if you utilize a ramp, you must build twelve inch of ramp length for every one inch of height to the porch landing. This decision may also be affected by the climate where you reside.

In addition to the ramp or lift, once you arrive at the porch level, you will need to consider the next hazard of the actual threshold to enter the home. Most homes have either a step up into the residence or a one-to-three-inch-high threshold barrier to crossover. There are many exterior small threshold ramps adjustable in height allowing a safe entrance into the home.

2. Doorways

Once in the home, many things are required for immediate safety along with considerations for longer term solutions. Inside the home, the most important need is making the doorways wide enough (minimum is thirty-two inches) to accommodate a wheelchair. If wheelchair accessibility is not immediately required, doorway changes should always be considered as a long-term solution. Even if you are not returning from an injury, walkers/rollators often become a necessity as we age to assist us with our mobility. Narrow doorways always become an obstacle in the future.

3. Decluttering

Another vital change in the home, regardless of an illness, is what I explain to my clients as "Tidy Up." The concept is decluttering by using four elements: keep, donate, sell, and pass on/share. Any home is not a safe environment if you have clutter and debris limiting accessibility throughout the home. When losing our balance, we tend to grab for anything. Clutter is unable to support your weight and can result in a fall. The outcome is a potential hospital visit or an injury requiring a long-term recovery. Falls are the leading cause of injury related deaths in seniors.

4. First Floor Bathroom

The most important modification is to make a first-floor bathroom accessible for safe toileting and showering. Safe seating options, along with a handheld shower head, are required for a spouse or caregiver. For a long-term condition, a roll-in shower is required to maintain a level of independence as well as proper healthy grooming habits. If the home can accommodate a first-floor bathroom, consider converting a dining room or den into a bedroom to avoid climbing stairs throughout the home. If a first-floor bathroom is not an option, a stair lift is highly recommended to limit a fall when ascending or descending the stairs. You can also create a "walk-in" or "roll-in" shower for the second-floor bathroom.

5. Other Modifications

Some other modifications might include a first-floor laundry area, lighted pathways to safely guide you to bathrooms at night, proper counter heights in both the bathrooms and kitchen to accommodate wheelchair accessibility.

Wayne Mitchell:

Assistance with caregiving to support both a loved one and the family may be necessary. If that is the case, there are three specific questions you should think about.

What help can a caregiver provide?

Caregivers provide a broad array of assistance and services based on their experience and the plan of care that is developed between the family and a healthcare professional (such as a physician, registered nurse, or home care consultant). In-home caregiver service is distinct from home health or professional services. These services are "skilled," meaning they are provided by a registered nurse (RN), licensed practical nurse (LPN), physical therapist (PT), occupational therapist (OT) and speech therapist (ST), to name a few.

By contrast, an in-home caregiver may have basic care training, a personal care aid certificate (PCA), or certified nurse assistant (CNA), with many states having licensing requirement for CNAs. The differences in each may be the type of training they received, number of classroom and clinic hours, in-person or online classes, the facilitator's training, their prior experience, and receipt of a certificate of completion or a state license.

These caregivers generally provide services that fall under the title of Activities of Daily Living (or ADLs). This is a term used to describe the fundamental skills required to care for oneself and is usually broken down into two categories: Basic Activities of Daily Living and Instrumental Activities of Daily Living. During an assessment of the person needing care, these life skills are evaluated to develop a plan of care the caregiver will follow.

Basic Activities of Daily Living (BADL) are skills that manage a person's basic physical needs, such as:
• Dressing
• Personal hygiene
• Toileting
• Eating
• Transferring from a chair to a bed or commode
• Walking or moving around the home

Instrumental Activities of Daily Living (IADL) are more complex activities that allow a person to live independently, such as:
• Preparing meals
• Taking medications
• Shopping
• Able to manage finances
• Laundry
• Housekeeping
• Using the telephone

Other services a caregiver can provide are: bathing, light housekeeping, transportation, errand service, picking up medications, attending medical appointments, respite service, and companionship. The caregiving services are part of the plan of care established by you, your family, healthcare professional, or home care specialist and based upon the assessment and your personal requests.

What caregiver types are available?

Many types of caregivers are available: family, community members, or a hired caregiver service. When deciding on a caregiver option, each has pros and cons that should be considered. These may affect the care provided, tax and insurance liabilities, and financial viability.

A discussion with your tax advisor, attorney, and insurance agent is often overlooked but it is a potentially critical step in deciding the best choice for the individual needing care.

Here are examples of pros and cons for each type of caregivers:

1. Family Members

Could be immediate family such as spouse, son, daughter, sister, and brother. Or extended family such as grandchildren, and in-laws.

Pros
- No or low cost
- You know them and are comfortable with them in your home
- They understand your wants, needs and personality
- May have more flexible scheduling
- Dependable

Cons
- Little to no experience
- May have their own schedules to work around
- For prolonged periods may exhibit exhaustion or burn out
- May be uncomfortable providing personal care

2. Friends or Neighbors

Typically, these people are close friends or friendly neighbors who the individual and family know.

Pros
- No or low cost
- You know them but may be uncomfortable with them in your home

Cons
- Little to no experience
- Usually have set schedules to work around
- May be undependable
- Can have multiple people coming and going
- May be uncomfortable performing personal care
- Loss of privacy

3. Social Service or Church Volunteers

Contact social service agencies such as county council on aging, county social service department, local churches, homeowners' association, senior service center, local senior service associations.

Pros
- Little to no cost
- Some volunteers may have experience in caregiving

Cons
- Unable to meet your needs and schedule
- Not knowing the person or persons coming into your home
- Loss of privacy

4. Independent Hire Caregiver

Found on job boards, classified ads, bulletin board postings, word of mouth.

Pros
- Usually has experience but may not have formal training
- Can work around your needs and schedules
- Mostly dependable
- May have references

Cons
- Cost usually not covered by typical health insurance
- Unknown individual and background, requires trust in a stranger
- You need to manage and supervise
- If they are unable to be there one day, you may not have anyone

- Usually not insured for liability or injury
- Tax and employer liabilities since you are hiring them; check with a tax advisor
- Personal liability - check with your insurance agent to see if your insurance policies cover having a paid person working in your home, since you may be considered an employer

5. Home Health Care Company

If you are being discharged from a hospital or rehabilitation facility, they will usually suggest a home health care company to provide skilled nursing services, sometime referred to a visiting nurse. Although caregiver is not their primary service, they may be able to recommend a caregiver.

Pros
- They are known by the facility
- Licensed
- Insured
- Trained staff

Cons
- Caregiver services are usually not covered by insurance
- The caregiving is usually ancillary to the skilled services being provided

6. Home Care Agency

If you are being discharged from a hospital or rehabilitation facility, they may recommend a home care agency. You can find them in publications, online, or through local senior service agencies, physician offices, and word of mouth.

Pros

- Their main focus is providing in-home caregiving services
- Staff is trained and usually certified in providing caregiving services
- Most agencies verify references, work history, certifications, and perform a criminal background check
- Caregivers are typically employees of the home care agency and would be covered under the agency insurance, including liability and workers compensation
- No tax liabilities concerns
- Flexible scheduling and should provide services even if the regular caregiver is unable to work
- No need to supervise the caregiver as the agency supervises the caregiver

Cons

- Cost is usually higher due to agency expenses, management, insurance, etc.
- Cost is usually not covered by typical health insurance
- May have minimum scheduling requirements

Where can you find out about the type of caregiving needs required?

The first step in determining caregiver needs is meeting with a healthcare provider or physician. This discussion should be honest and open; it should include challenges such as being unstable when walking, forgetfulness, and difficulty with personal hygiene and care, just to name a few. The healthcare provider should be able to make recommendations or at the very least refer you to a home care specialist.

When making the decision about care, look for some of these signs which may be indicators that help should be considered:
• Decline in personal hygiene/care
• The person seems depressed or talks about feeling lonely
• Cleanliness of the home has deteriorated/trash not being emptied
• Lack of food/spoiled food in the refrigerator

In many cases, home health care starts with family and friends helping to "pick up the slack." However, if looking after an older adult with more complex concerns, a professional in-home caregiver can be considered.

Invite a few home care agencies to the house to meet with the individual needing care and the family. Many will do a free assessment and make a recommendation of the specific caregiving needs, based on their activities of daily living. Ask the home care agency if the person doing the assessment is a skilled healthcare professional such as a nurse, trained home care consultant, or case manager.

When deciding on an independent hire caregiver or home care agency, an in-home assessment is important. The healthcare professional can see firsthand the living environment and personal interactions.

One of the major purposes of having an in-home caregiver is for safety and security. I often also prioritize a home safety assessment. This will help point out the physical safety concerns in and around the home such as trip and fall hazards, proper lighting, safe and clear entry and exit pathways, handrails, grab bars, torn or loose carpeting, and throw rug or doormats that may slip underfoot. Sometimes, a specialized safety assessment may be indicated depending on specific concerns, such as the safety of an individual with Alzheimer's Disease or memory issues.

When first starting, you may not know what questions to ask. I have prepared a list of questions that should be asked by every independent hire caregiver and home care agency. Scan this QR code for my questionnaire, "What questions should I ask when interviewing a caregiver or home care agency?" Ask these questions to everyone you are considering for caregiving services in the home. This will provide better insight with your decision-making process and help to find the best fit for the situation.

Carmen Perry-Tevaga:

Staying socially connected while recovering at home plays a role in the healing process. Here are some ideas to consider when settling into a routine for a safer and good recovery.

When you're dealing with all the chaos of navigating back to your home after an acute stay, the last thing on your mind is staying connected. Let's face it, when you're in a hospital or skilled facility, all you do is connect... with your nurses, caregivers, social workers, discharge planners, home health companies, the on-site physician and sometimes your roommates.

What often happens when you discharge home is a honeymoon period. You are thankful that no one is poking and prodding you all hours of the night. There are no beeping alarms from machines up and down the halls. It is just you and your peaceful, quiet home. Once the excitement of escaping the grasp of institutional living has subsided, you will experience a sense of loneliness. You will feel a desire to connect to those you care about and those who care about you.

When I was on a work trip in St. Louis, I got the call that my mother had been admitted to the hospital. Of course, all the familiar questions ran through my head like, what happened? Is she responsive? Or what could I have done to prevent this? It's a terrible call to get. It became painfully clear that my mom needed a better way to stay in contact with me. Yes, my mother had a cell phone, but for some reason it was never functioning properly. It was the screen, or the camera, or the speaker. The list went on and on. There was something always wrong with her perfectly good cell phone.

Fortunately, my mother recovered from that hospital stay and returned to her home. At work we were piloting a new system called Smart Companion. My mother was one of our first clients. It is a voice activated medical alert system with the benefits and entertainment of an Amazon Alexa device.

When the system arrived in the box, the first instruction was to call the customer support team to walk through a very simple set up. The second instruction was to test the Emergency Response System by making a test call. I will never forget what my mother said to me after making that call. She said, "It just gives me peace of mind." For someone who just discharged from a 3-month Skilled Nursing stay, it was all that I could ask for.

My mom quickly started utilizing this Smart Companion to video call her children and grandchildren. She immediately was able to feel connected to her coast-to-coast support system. She would use the system to play Hawaiian music, which she loved to listen to. It reminded her of a trip she took with her best friend to Kauai. She would set reminders, ask it questions, but most of all she used it to connect.

It is a basic human need to feel connected, but the reality is that it is becoming increasingly difficult to do if you aren't familiar with commonly used technology. There are so many options different systems and options for connecting. My advice when looking for what will be the best fit for your family is consider who is using the system and whom they need to connect to. Do not overwhelm anyone with overbearing monitoring or complicated technology. Make sure if you try something and it doesn't work, don't be afraid to try something else. Nothing is one size fits all.

Question 3: *I live alone and have no children. I enjoy my home and keep busy with my interests. Is it okay for me to stay in my home? Are there things I should do to better manage aging in place?*

Amy Miller:

Solo seniors are the largest growing age demographic, based on the 2020 United States Census; 20 percent of those over the age of 55 are not married or have children. If you find yourself in this situation, you are not alone. The good news is that you can enjoy your retirement and surround yourself with the people you love doing things you want to do.

I met a man in his '60s named Rick, and he shared with me that he was sent home after fourteen days in the hospital following a heart attack per Medicare guidelines. He struggled with meals and taking his medication as he recuperated. Since Rick lived alone, he had not planned to ask for extended family or friends to stop by to check on him or provide food. Rick was not well enough to grocery shop; he relied on fast food deliveries or did not eat.

Living alone as you age becomes a concern as isolation and personal safety might be at risk. Those who live alone may not receive any feedback that they are showing signs of declining abilities. Slips, trips, and falls are a leading indicator that older people need a higher level of care.

Financial exploitation and elder abuse concern many older adults who age alone. Finding a trusted network of advisors and friends is imperative. Consider bringing in a neutral, third party to oversee your plan to provide some protection and accountability, from the planning stages through the closure of your estate. No one should be going through aging and end of life alone.

Staying active and engaged is the best solution for anyone who lives alone. Volunteering for your favorite cause, taking classes, working out or going for daily exercise gives you something to look forward to every day. Many older adults choose to start a business, work part-time to make extra money, or spend time with younger people to stay active.

Write down and pay for your plans. A growing number of older people are creating a caregiving agreement for loved ones so they know what to do in an emergency and what they would be paid for providing the services. Consider the gifting clause allowed by the IRS (up to $16,000 per person per year) to compensate others for providing care and services tax free. This helps your trusted advisors to carry out your wishes so they know what is important to you.

Create a daily plan to check in with someone. I know of several older adults who have an agreement to text or Facebook family or friends every morning by 10 a.m. to check in. They usually send a bit of news or a funny meme they found online. If they do not hear from one another, they will send a note or swing by their home to personally check in on them.

If housing is a concern, some Solo Seniors consider having a young family member move into their home and provide home maintenance in lieu of lower rent. Home sharing companies are popping up to locate potential roommates. A friend of mine told me about how her father remodeled his one level rambler into a two-suite home for him to rent out a portion of his home. Other options include 55+ apartment communities, extended stay hotels, or RV parks where others are around to help in the event of an emergency.

AREAS TO CONSIDER

Choice of Residence
1. Are you comfortable in your current residence?
2. Do you want to remain in your current residence?
3. If you are not comfortable in your present residence, what would you prefer?
   - Downsizing to something smaller
   - Something less expensive
   - Prefer one-story living
   - A residence better suited for my physical condition
   - Better accessibility to family/friends
   - A different climate
   - Better accessibility to transportation
   - Better accessibility to culture and entertainment
   - Other (Explain)
4. In assessing your living conditions, what are the things you must have? What are the things you have, but could live without?

Affordability

1. What percentage of your monthly income is your mortgage/rent and fixed living expenses?
2. Do you have enough money remaining to meet your other needs?

Comfort & Accessibility

1. Can you comfortably move around your home?
2. What home technology have you explored to promote aging in place?
   - Smart phones
   - Tablets and computers
   - Video monitoring systems
   - Non-intrusive monitoring systems
   - Medical Alert Monitoring

For more Areas to Consider related to the Housing Pillar, download the *Act III: Your Plan for Aging in Place* at https://naipc.memberclicks.net/ or scan the QR code:

Pillar 2: Health and Wellness

 Part of our life's journey is aging, and with that comes changes in our overall health. The secret to enjoying our daily life as we enter our later decades is to plan ahead so we are safe, as independent as possible, and active, however that is defined for you. It comes down to understanding our choices, deciding what we want our health (body, mind, and spirit) to be, and what resources are available to help us achieve whatever goals we make for ourselves.

The questions we address in "Pillar 2: Health and Wellness" are designed to get you thinking about what you want your health and wellness life to be. Keep in mind, it does not matter whether you are just starting out or amid managing a crisis situation in your life at the moment, it is *never* too late to make your aging in place plans for your health and wellness.

Read what our experts share about tools and resources available so you and your family are comfortable with the idea of you aging in your home.

Question 1: *I live on my own and can take care of myself. My children don't accept that I can manage things on my own at home. What can I do to make them feel comfortable with me remaining at home on my own?*

Ryan McEniff:

Different types of in-home assistance exist today to help older adults maintain their independence. In addition, there are specific actions you can take to feel safe and more comfortable living on your own. You will find the following information helpful as you prepare for aging successfully in place.

There are two main types of in-home care services for older adults: private home care and Medicaid home care.

1. Private Home Care

Private home care is either paid for out-of-pocket or through a long-term care insurance policy. A home care agency will match the right caregiver to your care needs and desired schedule. Depending on the complexity of the case or the scheduled hours needed, your rate quote may change.

A great resource is the "Genworth Cost of Care Study," which shows families the likely cost of care in each state and region of the state. Visit https://www.genworth.com/aging-and-you/finances/cost-of-care.html or scan the QR code below:

Expect a required minimum hours per week and per shift. If possible, keep the same schedule each week. This allows you to have continuity of caregivers; the more changes to the schedule, the less consistency you will receive.

The benefit of working with an agency is that their office staff assists with scheduling, including call-outs and ensuring high-quality care is provided. You also do not need to worry about insurance, taxes, and mandatory benefits as caregivers are employed by the agency directly.

The downside is these benefits can lead to more expensive services. Expect the cost of care to continue to increase as staffing is challenging and competitive.

2. Medicaid Home Care

The second option available is Medicaid home care. This is generally provided by a home care agency that has a contract with Medicaid to provide in-home care to low-income seniors.

Typically, these types of services are shorter visits a few times a week, and they are task focused. There are usually long-wait times and caregivers can be inconsistent, depending on the number of caregivers an agency has available.

In-home care helps older adults maintain as much independence as possible while allowing them to stay in their own home and prevents an unwanted move into a care facility. As an individual's health and cognition declines, the amount of care can be increased.

Other Benefits of In-Home Care

Dementia and fall prevention are the top two reasons why a family decides to hire in-home care services, but there are many other reasons why people hire caregivers. Some of the tasks caregivers are typically hired to provide are:

• Ambulation
• Feeding
• Bathing
• Dressing
• Personal Hygiene
• Continence
• Toileting
• Laundry
• Meal Preparation

For older adults who are not in need of in-home care but are contemplating how to stay safely in their home, I would recommend considering some basic home modifications for fall prevention.

Grab bars are a low-cost option to keep an older adult from falling. Install them whenever possible, but especially in showers, bathrooms, and short stairways. For long stairways, it is beneficial to install a weight-bearing handrail, as many handrails are merely decorative.

Consider installing a shower chair, low-profile tub, and a hand-held shower head to make bathing easier and safer.

Remember, *an ounce of prevention is worth a pound of cure.*

Use of Technology

Another popular route is using a remote monitoring system. The most well-known are Personal Emergency Responses Systems (PERS) devices. You may recall the phrase, "Help I've fallen and can't get up!"

Technology continues to become more sophisticated. The days of needing to wear and press a button are coming to an end. Remote monitoring systems are becoming so advanced that they not only can detect a fall without a camera, but they can collect health analytics that family members and doctors utilize to make informed decisions about their loved-one's care.

These systems cater to older adults who want to stay in their homes without the expensive cost of home care services and allow adult children to understand how their parents are doing, regardless of where they live.

Deanne O'Rear Cameron:

Good and honest communication with children and other family members is essential when you want to age in place. Let's consider some basic recommendations to help improve communication as well as the best way to manage potential disagreements.

When communicating with children or family that you can take care of yourself, share why you feel you can live on your own. Let them know any information or services that you have already put in place or are researching for possible future needs. This will help ensure them that you are taking proper steps and understand what is necessary to take care of yourself as you age in place. If your family lives out of town, let them know you have friends and neighbors who will check on you. They should know when these people will be utilized. Get their permission to share their contact information with your family.

If disagreements should arise, calmly discuss the reason behind the dispute. Find out why they disagree by asking questions. Help them to understand any misconceptions they may have about your situation, but also listen to their responses. Their point of view may be something you had not thought of. Being open-minded can help you work through it.

If anything poses a danger to living on your own and taking care of yourself, address it swiftly. Keep your family involved so they see you are taking necessary steps to remain where you are. This will also give them confidence you will be proactive at living safely on your own.

My own situation with family taught me to be understanding. It was important to appreciate why my loved one wanted to live on her own as long as possible. Assisting her with finding resources based on the wants and needs she expressed helped her remain independent. Some of her desires seemed over the top until I was reminded how I want to live.

When talking to your family, be sure to ask them how they would want to live. It is a way to help direct the conversation and lead you down the path to better communication and agreement.

Ronnie Genser:

There can be different methods of communicating with family members or friends about the desire to age in place. Plus, there are many resources available for you to enjoy the experience of living an independent lifestyle at home. Let's review some ideas by answering a few questions.

How do I communicate with my children that I am okay?

I suggest you call a family meeting where you can all be together at the same time, either in the same physical place or via Zoom. Ask them, one-by-one, for specifics as to why they feel you cannot manage things in your own home. As each person communicates their thoughts, be sure to take detailed notes without responding to them at this time.

When you feel your adult children have communicated all their thoughts as to why you can't manage on your own, read back to each one what they said to confirm you have understood them correctly.

Using your own notes, calmly address each of their concerns one by one, most importantly with specifics. If one or more of your adult children still seem concerned or have questions, ask each person for more specific information, so you can address their remaining concerns.

Are there actions I should take to make them feel comfortable?

Yes. Make sure you are very specific in your response, and if possible, provide more than one example that addresses each concern.

What resources are available for me to enjoy independence at home?

There are a number of resources available to you. Let me highlight some ideas below:

1. Nonprofit Volunteer
Ask friends and/or use the internet to learn about volunteer opportunities that can be done at home. Also, contact organizations like Hands On Atlanta (https://www.handsonatlanta.org/). Even though this organization is based in Atlanta, Georgia, ask about

volunteer opportunities that can be done remotely at home using your phone or computer.

2. Local Politics Volunteer

Several months prior to a local or national election, call your favorite candidate's office and ask if they have any volunteer opportunities you can do at home.

3. Educational Opportunities

Investigate local and national educational and technology opportunities on the internet. Many are specifically designed for older adults, such as:

a) States, such as Georgia, offer free college courses for residents sixty-two years old and above, at colleges and universities in their state system.

b) Older Adults Technology Services (OATS) (https://oats.org) from AARP. Their Senior Planet, OATS' flagship program, (https://seniorplanet.org/about/who-is-oats/) provides both new learning and enjoyment at home.

c) National Resource Center for Osher Lifelong Learning Institutes (https://sps.northwestern.edu/oshernrc/resources/lifelon g-learning/)

4. AARP

Search the home page on AARP's website (www.aarp.org) for additional suggestions on engaging activities.

5. Group Travel

Explore group travel websites such as Road Scholar (www.roadscholar.org). It provides ideas and opportunities to explore places to visit with other older adults. You can also enjoy expanding new horizons.

6. Online Exercise Group

Join an online exercise group or see if there is an exercise group in your neighborhood, subdivision, condominium, or even cul-de-sac, to not only provide you with consistent exercise but the possibility of meeting new people who you might not otherwise have met.

7. Neighborhood and/or Association Meetings

If you are interested in meeting new people in your neighborhood or condominium association, attend neighborhood or condominium meetings. Is there a committee that interests you? Consider getting involved and enjoy meeting new people with common interests.

8. Online Games

A friend of mine, who used to play Mah-Jongg (https://en.wikipedia.org/wiki/Mahjong) every week in person with friends, now continues to play every week with them via the Real Mah Jongg website (https://realmahjongg.com/)
or via the app. She also suggested playing Words with Friends (https://wordswithfriends.com/) as another online option.

If any of these or other games is of interest you, invite other friends to play with you. Join an existing group who plays games online, or offer to fill in for someone in your group or another group who is unable to attend that week.

9. Religious Services Using Technology

Continue to attend religious services. Watch live-streaming from your religious institution on YouTube. Do they meet via Zoom? It provides an opportunity to see your friends and still feel part of your faith community.

Whatever choices you make to spend your time, be certain they are activities you look forward to doing, not just to fill time. If you find you are not enjoying something, make a change. Choose a different group or activity that brings you pleasure.

Question 2: *A main concern of individuals aging in place is falling. How can I create greater safety at home? Is decluttering my home an important first step to avoiding falls? What does this involve? What if I need help?*

Deanne O'Rear Cameron:

Slips and falls are the main cause of injury while aging in place in the home. The Centers for Disease Control and Prevention (CDC) reports that one in three older adults (age sixty-five and older) fall each year. Two-thirds of those who fall will fall again. This information is not to alarm you, but to help you prevent accidents in your home, which is where most falls occur.

Falls are the most common cause of traumatic brain injuries. The good news is that many falls are preventable, and you can reduce your risk of falling. None of us wants to think we are at that stage where we may start to have falls. In our mind we are fine and overlook the signs and preventative measures we can take. Many risk factors contribute to falls: medical conditions, balance impairment, muscle weakness, inadequate diet and exercise, vision and hearing impairment, and medications.

To combat these risks, let's look at some preventable measures:

1. Find a good balance and exercise program by contacting local area agencies on aging, community centers, and more, depending on your area. Walking, dancing, and Tai Chi are just a few examples of exercise.

2. Talk to your healthcare provider for a potential assessment of your risk of falling. Share any recent falls you may have had along with any dizzy spells.

3. Keep your home safe by decluttering your space. Although you may love your collectibles and throw rugs, these are often overlooked as a fall risk. When moving about near our treasures, we tend to be overly cautious and cause ourselves to lose balance so as to not touch them. Throw rugs can cause us to catch a toe and trip over them, so making sure they are secured is best.

4. Regularly review your medications with your doctor or pharmacist as they may have side effects that increase your risk of falling. When you pick-up your medication, make certain to review them with the pharmacist at the consultation window. Many people will skip this step. If you have your medications delivered, be sure you have this conversation with the pharmacist by phone. It is very important to know what you are taking and what to expect.

5. Have your vision and hearing checked annually. Update your eyeglasses and hearing aids, if you wear them. These can be a major cause of imbalance. People with a mild hearing loss (25 decibels) are nearly three times more likely to fall. People who have experienced ear infections may notice that their balance can be impacted.

If you enjoy walking outdoors, here are a few tips to reduce your risk of falling:

1. Watch for cracks in sidewalks, pot holes, tree roots, and changes in elevation (such as at crosswalks). Use ramps where possible.

2. Wear shoes with firm soles and low heels.

3. Walk in good lighting conditions where you can see the best.

4. Bring a friend so you can alert each other of potential hazards.

5. Use caution when carrying something. It can throw your balance off.

6. Always use handrails when they are available such as on public transportation or stairs.

These are a few proven strategies to keep you on your feet. Falls can happen at any age. So, everyone should practice these tips since falling is not just an aging issue.

Sue Haviland:

Maybe you are reading this question because a family member or friend took a bad fall resulting in injury or worse. Perhaps you have fallen and are concerned about falling again. You are not alone.

Safety in the home is a critical part of any aging in place plan, and discussion around fall prevention plays an important role. It's important to know that falls are not a normal part of aging, and many falls are preventable. Falls are among the top reasons for older adult hospital admissions. According to the Centers for Disease Control and Prevention (CDC), in 2019 falls were the leading cause of death from injury for older adults. Just one fall can completely derail even the best aging in place plan. Keep in mind, if someone is falling, there is a reason. We need to identify the reason(s) and take steps to deal with it. Here are a few possibilities:

1. Medication

Medication interaction and side-effects can cause a fall. Everyone should keep a current list of medications (prescription and over-the-counter) with them and bring it to each doctor visit. Keep a copy of that same list (updated as needed) in the home where it can be easily located in case of emergency. Your local pharmacist can be a resource when discussing medications and side-effects, including dizziness, drowsiness, etc.

2. Medical Conditions

Underlying medical conditions such as Parkinson's disease and diabetes can lead to falls. A stroke can cause balance issues that make falling more likely. We often think of high blood pressure being a concern, but low blood pressure can be dangerous, too.

3. Footwear

Footwear can pose a threat. Ill-fitting or worn-out footwear should be discarded in favor of something with support, is slip resistant, and lightweight. I happen to live in Southwest Florida. Yes, it's a flip-flop world, but they are not the best choice of footwear when it comes to fall prevention.

4. Assistive Devices

Even assistive devices, which are supposed to help us be stable, can pose a problem. If they are not fitted and used properly, a device can present a fall hazard.

We are talking about aging in place in our homes and that is where the nearly 60 percent of falls occur. Did you know that 70 percent of the falls happen in the bathroom? Such things as throw rugs, stairs, and even pets, can pose a tripping hazard. A few years ago, I helped my ninety-one-year-old mom look through every room in her house to identify fall or tripping hazards. It was eye-opening.

Why is it important to identify the reasons for falls? First, so actions can be taken to mitigate the risk. Second, you want to be sure that the home itself is suitable for an older adult to age in place. The good news is there are some simple, low-cost steps someone can take to make the home safer. In many cases, it is not necessary to spend a lot of money. Here are some ideas:

1. Bathroom
• Place non-slip mats in the tub and shower.
• Install lift bars next to low toilets.
• Have grab bars professionally installed in the shower

2. Kitchen
• Keep the floor clean and clutter free. Remove throw rugs, which can pose a tripping hazard.
• Anything other than a non-slip mat has got to go!
• Store commonly used items on lower shelves within easy reach.
• Use step stools with extended handles. Never use a chair to reach a high object.

3. Lighting
• Stairs should be lit at the top and bottom. Chances are if someone is going to fall on the stairs, it will be on the first or last step.
• Install motion activated night lights in the bedroom, bathroom, and hallways. No one should cross a dark room to use the bathroom in the middle of the night.
• All outside stairways and walkways should be well lit.

4. Stairs
• Handrails on all staircases are a must.

5. Throw Rugs

• Check every room in the house for slippery throw rugs and remove these from the home.

If renovations are needed in the home, consider consulting with a Certified Aging in Place Specialist (CAPS) contractor. Someone with this designation is knowledgeable about modifications you can make to help stay in your home safely and securely.

Keep in mind, many changes are simple and will not break the bank. If a more significant project is called for, (installing a chair lift or elevator, for example) there are many ways to cover these costs. Options include using your own assets, local grants, or a reverse mortgage. The bottom line is this - being proactive about preventing falls can help you keep that aging in place plan - *in place.*

Andriana Mendez:

A major contributing factor of aging in place is maintaining safety and function throughout your home. At this point, you may not want to rebuild your home from scratch. However, there are many things you can do that can greatly impact your home's fit for your needs. The goal is to see older adults such as yourself live out your years happy, healthy, and with the ability to do the activities you love each day without injury.

While no one ever anticipates they will fall at home, a fall can prove to be devastating to both an individual and to their families. For adults over the age of sixty-five, this is the leading cause of death. Plus, many older adults reduce their daily activities due to fear of falling again. I have seen how something as simple as tripping on a rug can cause drastic long-term lifestyle changes on a client's life. The emotional strain that follows a fall is, in some ways, worse than the fall itself. I have also seen people lose confidence in once-beloved activities because of this anxiety.

Many circumstances can cause a fall, such as an existing health condition or side-effects from medication. However, there are simple actions you can take around the home to reduce hazards. Here is a quick list of common household items that people tend to overlook that can be adjusted with little effort or financial investment:

- Rugs: Tape down edges that have curled up. Alternatively, add thin no-slip pads underneath.
- Cords: Tie back or tape all electrical cords so they are not loose on the floor.
- Clutter: Remove all items from the walkways that are potential tripping hazards. Some examples include shoes, pet supplies, literature, laundry, etc. Always keep walkways clear.
- Low Furniture: Push these up against walls and/or remove them from general open walk areas as to avoid being overlooked.
- Lighting: Add additional adhesive lights or brighter bulbs to poorly lit areas throughout the home and hallways.
- Accessibility: Move daily essentials, such as clothing and toiletries, within reach to avoid reaching for these items and losing your balance.

• Shower: Add non-slip grips to the shower and/or consider getting a shower chair.

Although requiring more of a budget, some important updates can have a tremendous effect on your safety. These include:

• Replacing or repairing buckled, uneven flooring and carpet.
• Installing grab bars in bathrooms.
• Installing railings or ramps on walkways outside the home or near stairs.
• Replacing a bath-tub style shower with a walk-in shower.

We spend a great deal of our business helping older adults and their families declutter living spaces to reduce fall risks in their homes. We recently visited a home where boxes were stacked along the hallway walls. Being a tight fit, a box could be easily knocked with an elbow. In a blink of an eye, a box could be under foot and result in a fall. We removed those boxes, condensed the content into clear totes, and placed them on waist-high shelves in the guest bedroom. This simple action allowed the client to not only have a better idea of what they had in the boxes, but cleared their hallway for a safer passage.

Consider inviting a third-party moving and hauling professional, organizer, or home health expert to visit your home to assess it for aging in place safety. Many of us are connected to reputable resources to provide the services you need to safely enhance your living environment for longevity. Having a second set of eyes evaluating your everyday space can make all the difference!

Question 3: *I was recently diagnosed with a disease. How do I tell my family? How do I prepare personally?*

Gina Knight:

When a health event is unexpected, it can feel like an overwhelming crisis. There are a lot of details to manage that not only include the medical side, but how to best create a safe and comfortable environment if an older adult wishes to remain at home. When immediate actions are required, this is when managing the crisis comes into play.

Senior Crisis Management plays an important role when older adults learn about a critical medical diagnosis. How one defines a crisis can be subjective. It often feels different between the family and the individual going through the crisis. Sometimes the family can have significantly different feelings on the severity and the approach to how they will manage the next steps.

Let me share some actions I recommend to my clients that you may find helpful if a crisis should come your way:

1. Take Notes at Meetings

Depending on the diagnosis, I strongly recommend one family member be designated to be responsible for taking copious notes while meeting with the medical team on "what to expect" both from a short-term and long-term perspective. If a family member is not available to offer their time, it's important to consider hiring a Care Manager. It is imperative that proposed changes are discussed to enable the family and older adult to agree with the home changes designed to accommodate the individual's future happiness, safety, and lifestyle. Keep in mind, the older adult is experiencing a high-level of stress, fear, loss of independence, and potential lack of control of the future.

2. Long and Short-Term Planning

When a chronic disease, such as a heart-attack occurs, older adults plan for a short-term recovery examining temporary versus permanent home modifications. Yet, the approach to a long-term diagnosis such as Alzheimer's can often be a more complicated approach when planning the future.

Making changes to diet and exercise habits, along with adjustments in the home, need to be considered for both the short-term and long-term, depending on the age, mobility, and the medical diagnosis. Also please keep in mind only doctors can provide the guidelines on how slowly or rapidly a patient may decline. Thus, being prepared and aware of sudden changes are vital to a successful, safe, secure, and happy environment. In addition, identifying your professional team (i.e., doctors, attorneys, certified home modification specialist, therapists, etc.) is also a prerequisite component to any aging in place plan.

An example of a temporary modification may include renting an exterior metal ramp for the person unable to walk following a surgical procedure. Several other immediate short-term crisis solutions might include:

• Consider a wall hung shower seat, handheld shower head and grab bars in the showering area.

- Install a comfort height toilet with a stand-alone safety rail device, chair lift for upstairs/downstairs access, rolling tray table making eating easier during recovery, a power lift chair and an adjustable bed for the head and feet during the recovery process.

3. Alzheimer's or Other Dementia Diagnosis

The approach for a more progressive, long-term diagnosis such as Alzheimer's may often involve the following:

- Eliminate driving privileges. Driving is no longer safe for the older adult or others on the roads. This can be one of the most difficult conversations for both the individual and their loved ones.
- Switch from a gas stove to an induction stove to prevent fires in the kitchen. Older adults often forget they started cooking.
- Notify local police and fire departments a loved one is living at the home and they have received an Alzheimer's diagnosis. Police and fire will keep an eye out with knowledge of the type of individual living in the home during a potential emergency.
- Install proper locks and remote alarm notifications should your loved one wander during their decline.
- Provide medicine dispensers that precisely deliver medication, wearable life alert pendants, and in-home camera monitoring systems are additional options to consider.

As an older adult's particular disease progresses, it may become necessary to bring in a caregiver if they wish to remain in their home. Very often families find it more comforting, and certainly safer, transitioning their loved ones to a memory care community designed to protect their loved ones from wandering, falling, injuring themselves, along with a more organized, on-going social environment.

Question 4: *What can I do to develop better balance and physical conditioning so I can stay safe and independent at home?*

C. Vicki Gold, PT, MA:

The information I am going to share with you may be considered mind-body and well-being fitness because of their interconnected relationship. They work together to optimize your health and well-being instead of living with illness and disability.

The best results come when you make exercises and related techniques a part of your daily life and activities. The good news is you can develop mind-body fitness and well-being in the comfort of your own home. You do not need to attend a gym or have special equipment.

To begin, there are Functional Fitness activities we do every day: rolling over, sitting up and getting out of bed, standing from a chair and sitting back down, walking to another room, reaching up to comb our hair or get something off a high shelf, and bend down to pick up something.

After years of experience treating people as a licensed physical therapist, I created The ABC System - Align, Breathe, and Center - to give others the knowledge and skills to improve their physical and mental well-being.

Alignment

Alignment refers to your posture. The better your posture is, the better your body can function. I often tell the story of a former patient who was sitting, slouched in my waiting room. When I asked her what her problem was, she said, "I can't raise my arm up. It hurts." Since she was early for her appointment, I asked if I could reposition her in the chair; placed a rolled-up towel in the arch of her back; placed her arms on a pillow for support and asked her to focus on her breathing until I returned.

When I came back fifteen minutes later, she amazed us both when her arm flew straight up without a wince of pain.

So how can you too improve your alignment?

Try using mental imagery. Think "Lengthen-Open." Allow your chin to tuck and the back of your head rise. Let your shoulders drop down and back. As you do this, allow your chest to lift and expand and your back to arch slightly.

Sit in a chair that provides support to your back. Use a lumbar cushion or towel roll for additional support. Use arm rests or sit at a desk or table to assist for good postural alignment. In bed, try to avoid having too many pillows under your head, which can limit your breathing.

Breathing

Breathing is automatic, something we do without thinking. Practice conscious breathing. Maintain your good alignment and breathe in through your nose. Feel the air go down to your belly region.

Next, allow your breath to come out slowly through pursed lips or make a hissing sound (s-s-s-s-s-s s-s). Try to blow out as slowly and as long as you can before breathing in again. This is an excellent technique for stress-reduction, pain management, and for increasing your respiratory capacity.

Centering

Centering is the ability to focus on one exercise or activity at a time. When you remain centered, it will help you avoid distractions, which can lead to falls, accidents, and injuries.

A useful strategy is to learn to "Start-Change-Stop." It means to consciously declare when you "Start" any activity. As you are doing the activity, no matter how large or small it may be, that is the "Change." When you finish the activity, you say or think "Stop."

For a free 15-minutes consultation to learn more about my ABC System, visit www.thera-fitness.com and complete the form on the home page.

Balance and Walking

Balance is a challenge for many of us as we age. As a result, people often develop a fear of falling.

Here are some tips you may find helpful:

- Get a medical workup for conditions like vertigo, which impacts your balance.
- Maintain the strength and flexibility of your hips, knees and especially feet.
- Practice slowly shifting your weight from side to side as you are in the semi-squatted position. Don't forget to stop in the center before changing sides.
- Practice balance skills in a doorway.

In all circumstances, you should have a responsible person available to help or supervise when doing exercises or activities that challenge your current abilities.

Get Up from the Ground

I understand not everyone can or should try to do this, but the ability to get down and safely up again from the ground is a good functional fitness exercise. If you can maintain or build up the ability, it will offer you more confidence and can be a valuable skill to retain as you age.

In addition to Functional Fitness activities, there are some practical actions you can do to avoid injury so you can enjoy better health and well-being.

Walking Considerations

Let's talk about footwear. No slippers or flip-flops, please. Always wear well-fitted and supportive shoes. Try shoes on at the end of the day as feet slightly swell over the course of the day. Make sure there is room at the end of your big toe and the wide part of your foot aligns with the wide part of the shoe when you are standing.

Properly fitted canes or walkers should always be used if needed for improved safety. Are you resistant to using these tools because you think they make you look old? Consider this point of view - using a walking aid can help you be safer, enjoy independence, and perhaps avoid the pain and inconvenience of injury.

Manage Fear of Falling

It is not unusual to develop a fear of falling if your balance is off, or if you have had at least one fall. Make certain to discuss your fear with your medical provider and/or physical therapist.

Let me share two strategies you may find helpful:

- Change your mind set by talking to the fear. Say to yourself, "I know you are there, but I am not going to let you be in charge!" A positive attitude towards a fear can provide a form of empowerment for you.
- Learn to use empowering self-talk. This strategy can be useful in any situation where fear is limiting your confidence about performing a task. A good self-talk statement is, "I am tall, strong, and confident." This kind of self-talk can work in almost any situation where your confidence needs a little boost, even if you're short.

Work with a Physical Therapist

Any physical therapist will provide an assessment of your medical and physical status, as well as the physical and social environment in which you function. They will work with you, your family member(s), or caregivers to establish goals and design a plan of activities to help you achieve those goals. A schedule of therapy sessions will be established and discharge plans arranged when the time comes. The American Physical Therapy Association (APTA) with its local chapters is a good resource.

AREAS TO CONSIDER

General Health and Wellness

1. What concerns do you have in particular about your health?
• Medical condition/chronic illness
• Chronic pain
• Limited mobility
• Costs of medical care
• Difficulty getting to medical appointments

2. Do you feel you have a sufficient understanding of the benefits provided by Medicare or private insurance?

3. Are your benefits enough to cover your medical costs?

4. If you answered "no" to questions 2 and 3, have you used benefitscheckup.org to determine if you might be eligible for additional medical benefits or programs?

Daily Living/In Home Care

1. Do you have a personal health record? Do you have a current list of medications, physicians, and health conditions?

If you answered "no," scan the QR code for a worksheet from AARP or visit the link at https://assets.aarp.org/www.aarp.org_/articles/learntech/wellbeing/medication-record.pdf

2. Have you considered home modifications that can be done to help address physical changes as you age or as brought about by a condition?

3. Have you researched technology products that might assist in managing your daily life?

For more Areas to Consider related to the Health & Wellness Pillar, download the *Act III: Your Plan for Aging in Place* at https://naipc.memberclicks.net/ or scan the QR code:

Pillar 3: Personal Finance

The "Pillar 3: Personal Finance" chapter turned out to be our most robust and information-packed section of the book. This makes sense, because our personal finances often dictate life's choices and decisions, including the other pillars discussed throughout the book.

If there is one fact that is true about personal finance, it is this: if these topics are not discussed, figured out, and action taken, the outcome of inaction can become a big problem. Our advice is to read through this chapter very slowly. The next step will be to identify who can be your support and guide so you can begin moving forward and making decisions that will protect your financial future.

Below are the main topics discussed in this chapter:

1. Financial Planning: Topics include financial abuse, account consolidation, blended families and finances, and power of attorney.

2. Medicare: This complex subject highlights Medicare Part A, B, C, and D, Medicare Advantage plans, Medicare penalties, Special Election Periods, Supplemental plans, and Veteran's Aid and Attendance Benefits.

3. Reverse Mortgages: Two authors address this topic, each bringing their insights to questions such as how a reverse mortgage works, types of reverse mortgages, and key points to decide if a reverse mortgage is for you.

4. Pension versus 401(k): A brief discussion talking about the difference between a 401(k) plan and a pension.

5. Hospice Care: We share two stories that provide a personal experience to better understand hospice care.

6. Funeral Planning: Find out funeral options, costs, options to cover the expense, steps to follow, working with a corporate-owned or family-owned funeral home, and the funeral benefit provided by Social Security.

> **Question 1:** *What costs do I need to consider, and what income sources are available whether I move to a community or remain in my home?*

Julianne Rizzo, RN, MBA, CSA:

The basic concept in the cost of senior living is assistance with Activities of Daily Living (ADLs). These activities are bathing, feeding yourself, getting dressing, transferring in and out of sitting position, toileting, and continence. Any community you are considering will do a "Needs Assessment" and determine what ADLs you need assistance with and how much assistance. Based on that assessment they will give you a monthly cost!

How Will You Pay for It?

The most misunderstood idea of senior living is that Medicare will cover senior living expenses. Medicare pays for hospitalization, temporary skilled nursing, doctor visits, and medication. It can also pay for equipment like a wheelchair. However, Medicare will not pay for long-term care living expenses in a community. Think of it like this - does Medicare currently pay your rent?

Monthly Income

We start by looking at your monthly income. Below are a few types of income to take into your calculations:

- Social Security (also known as SSN)
- Disability insurance (also known as SSDI)
- IRA and annuity monthly payout
- Pensions

Long-Term Care Insurance

Long-term care insurance is a great benefit that individuals purchase to help pay for care as they age. It can often be pricey for individuals, and the later in life you sign up for it the more expensive it will be.

Each policy includes criteria under which they will pay for care. Typically, it is when the older adult needs assistance with two or more ADLs. Some policies will pay for care only in a community that is staffed 24/7 by registered nurses and some policy you can get services at home.

Some policies have clauses of when financial assistance can start, such as after 30 days services have been introduced. Know what the requirements and stipulations are for any policy before you sign up.

Veterans Benefits

The Veterans Benefits Administration offers tax-free, monthly monetary payments to certain wartime veterans with financial need and their survivors. The VA revised the rules for eligibility in 2021 and is income and asset based.

The first requirement is serving at least one day during wartime:

- World War II: December 7, 1941-December 31, 1946
- Korean Conflict: June 27, 1950-January 31, 1955
- Vietnam Era: August 5, 1964-May 7, 1975
- Persian Gulf War: August 2, 1990 - date to be prescribed by Presidential Proclamation or law

The second requirement is that you have a net worth lower than $138,439. A primary residence and auto are not counted as part of net worth. Ongoing non-reimbursable medical and long-term care expenses may reduce your countable income.

This is a tax-free benefit:
- Surviving Spouse: $1,318 monthly / $15,816 annually
- Married Veteran: $2,431 monthly / $29,175 annually

It is a challenge to file the paperwork on your own, so keep in mind the VA can provide you free assistance, or you can hire someone to do it for you for a nominal fee.

Using Medicaid for Senior Living

To qualify for Medicaid, income and assets must be below certain limits. The limit varies state-by-state and even county-by-county. I would check with your state's Medicaid eligibility website and application process.

The biggest confusion is there are a couple different types of Medicaid. Medicaid pays for your insurance or food stamps, and Medicaid, in some cases, will cover housing. Speaking with the right people can help clarify which you need.

Most assisted living and memory care communities never accept Medicaid under any circumstances. However, there are some communities that will accept Medicaid, but only after you have lived there for a period paying with private assets. This is called a "spend-down" period.

Question 2: *How do I choose a trustworthy financial planner?*

Mary Kay Furiasse, BSN, JD, LLM:

It's important to do your homework. As in any situation when researching a professional with whom you wish to work, start by asking your friends for referrals. Avoid the sales talk and check them out first.

Reputable financial planners, like most professionals, are subject to licensure and regulatory oversight. Ask them which agency provides their oversight. It should be either FINRA (Financial Industry Regulatory Authority) or the SEC (Securities and Exchange Commission). Also look for financial planners who hold the CFP (Certified Financial Planner) designation. Understand the different types of assets and credentials as they apply to investment, insurance, and retirement planning.

Identify your goals and then interview potential planners before picking the registered fiduciary whose strategies work with your goals. Determine whether they are paid directly by fees from you or by commissions of fees filtered through a broker-dealer. Understand that each type has its own strengths and weaknesses. The CFP Board offers a guide called *Questions To Ask When Choosing A Financial Planner.* See the Notes and Additional Resources at the end of the book for the link or scan here:

Question 3: *Mom and Dad have financial investments in different accounts and banks. As the grown children, we are concerned they are not closely tracking their finances. How can we access their accounts, if needed? What is the best way to begin?*

Mary Kay Furiasse, BSN, JD, LLM:

The best way to begin is to seek to understand and respect their system of organization. Ask to help coordinate and consolidate their investments. Remember, as long as Mom and Dad are competent, they remain in charge of their decision-making.

If they have not already done so, suggest that they allow you to access their accounts online. Recommend they consolidate under the oversight of a single dedicated financial advisor, an educated fiduciary who will put their interest first. Consolidating accounts can make their estate plan more effective.

Share with Mom and Dad your concerns and your desire to help. Make certain to understand what the law allows and does not allow. As part of the natural aging process, we begin to lose some of our financial acuity. Make sure that they have current Financial Powers of Attorney in place before a parent requires caregiving that affects his or her ability to communicate or make reasoned decisions.

Question 4: *How do I protect myself from financial fraud or abuse?*

Mary Kay Furiasse, BSN, JD, LLM:

Financial exploitation has been identified as one of the most prevalent forms of elder abuse and can take many forms. The victims are often overwhelmed by the situation and too embarrassed to admit the abuse. The possibility of being preyed upon by financial scammers becomes greater with physical health issues or cognitive impairments. It may be possible to reduce your risk by checking your credit reports regularly, using banking apps that require verification, and disputing inappropriate charges immediately. It's a good idea to organize your assets and debts. Make a list along with all your passwords.

One of the most common forms of financial fraud or abuse is when someone missuses the Power of Attorney for Property. The abuse occurs when the agent makes a decision or takes an action that is not in your best interest. They are not supposed to commingle assets, take your funds, or make decisions in their own interest. If you become incapacitated, POAs are not generally subject to oversight by the court or third party. That is why one of the best ways to protect yourself from financial fraud or abuse is to make sure that you name someone whom you trust and include a duty to account.

You need to make your selection very, very carefully - your agent needs to be completely trustworthy and informed. Communicate with your prospective agent about what is important to you. Discuss when you want them to step in and what signs to watch for. Don't forget to include your family and friends about your POA. Be wary of anyone who wants to be your new "best friend" and wants to help you manage your money. Undue influence has become a challenging legal issue once capacity begins to fade.

I have provided some helpful resources in the Notes and Additional Resources chapter at the end of the book.

Question 5: *I have a blended family. What is the best approach to keep peace in the family when it comes to my finances? If I wish to provide for everyone, how should I go about it?*

Mary Kay Furiasse, BSN, JD, LLM:

Divvying up an estate can be especially complicated in blended families. Also known as stepfamilies, the blended family is increasingly important to understand. It is crucial to understand all prior divorce agreements, any prenuptials, and to know the family dynamics. Without a plan, children from multiple relationships may not be treated as intended, and the interests of surviving spouses may be in direct conflict with those children.

With a traditional estate plan, that includes a trust and will, you can provide for the distribution of your assets in detail. A simple will can direct how most of your assets are to be distributed; but with most blended families, that isn't going to accomplish what you want to do with your money after you're gone. When building and legally securing your estate, a trust can be fundamental.

You not only have to decide who will inherit and how much, but you also must decide when, how, in what form, and if there are any terms and conditions that need to be met before the distribution is made to the beneficiaries. In a blended family, it's important to consider contingent beneficiaries if any of the primary beneficiaries predecease you. With a plan, you can determine what goes to the current spouse, if any, and what goes to any children from current or prior relationships, thus balancing the interests among children from prior marriages and stepchildren. It's a delicate and critical issue that must be considered.

Remember that retirement plans and life insurance are controlled by the beneficiary form you filled out when you opened the retirement plan account or bought the insurance policy, not by your will or trust. Effective estate planning can make a big difference to family well-being, both now and in the future.

Question 6: *What is the difference between capacity and competency? Why do I need a Power of Attorney (POA) to protect myself?*

Mary Kay Furiasse, BSN, JD, LLM:

Although capacity and competency are often used interchangeably, it's important to understand the difference, especially within the context of an individual's right to make their own decisions. All adults are presumed to be competent unless adjudicated otherwise by a court. Physicians can provide consultation and determine capacity; however, they cannot do so for competence. Capacity refers to someone's functional ability, while competence is determined by a judge, and is never determined by medical providers.

A power of attorney (POA), one of the core legal documents, and is the key to planning for incapacity and avoiding guardianship. A POA is empowered as the agent to act on your behalf, often avoiding the need for court involvement by seeking guardianship or conservatorship. You decide how much power to give your agent.

You must be mentally competent to engage the lawyer to create a POA. You can't create a POA after an injury or illness which prevents you from making your own decisions. As attorneys, we have ethical obligations to assure that the person understands the document at the time it is signed.

In most states, the standard of capacity is that for entering a contract they understand the terms of the agreement. The reality is, we are living longer, and as attorneys, we often deal with clients who have fading or diminished capacity.

If you have waited a bit too long to address estate planning documents, it may still be possible to sign legal documents with dementia but not incapacitated. Requisite capacity, even in advanced dementia cases, differs between medical incapacity and legal incapacity. Capacity requirements for each legal document may also vary and are determined by doctors.

Question 7: *What Is Medicare Part A, B, C, and D?*

Bonnie Dobbs:

Parts A and B are known as original Medicare. On the Medicare card, Part A is for Hospital and covers hospital, skilled nursing, home health care and hospice. Part B is for Medical. Part B covers doctors' services, medical supplies, tests, physical and speech therapy, and durable medical equipment.

Part C is another name for a Medicare advantage plan. Medicare Advantage plans are one of two ways to get coverage to offset the costs of what original Medicare does not pay. The other way to get coverage is a Medicare Supplement plan and a stand-alone drug plan. You must have both Part A and Part B to enroll in either of these two options.

Part D is a prescription drug plan. You can get drug coverage with a stand-alone plan which will have a monthly premium or by enrolling in an Advantage plan that includes drug coverage. The rules for Part D are the same for both options. They may have deductibles, but both have tier costs with copays or co-insurance, and the different coverage stages - initial coverage, donut hole or coverage gap, and catastrophic are the same.

Question 8: *When do I sign up to start Medicare?*

Bonnie Dobbs:

There are three times when one becomes Medicare eligible:

- When turning sixty-five years of age. You have a seven-month window, the three months prior to your sixty-fifth birthday, the month of and three months past.

- You have worked past age sixty-five, are now retiring, and you have a window of time to enroll in a plan. You must get coverage within eight months after losing employer coverage.

- You are under age sixty-five and have been on disability for twenty-four months. You become Medicare eligible in the twenty-fifth month and can enroll.

Medicare has various enrollment rules for each scenario. It is important to know these time frames and avoid incurring lifelong penalties.

Question 9: *Medicare can get a little complicated. Am I required to sign up for Medicare even if I have medical coverage with my current employer?*

Bonnie Dobbs:

Medicare has strict rules about when to enroll in the various parts. If your employer has at least twenty employees on company insurance, you can delay enrolling in Part B and Part D. If not, you must enroll in Part B and Part D when you become Medicare eligible or receive a penalty.

Here is a real-life situation: A woman with full credible coverage as a county school bus driver had been unnecessarily paying the Part B premium since turning 65. When she decided to retire, she discovered she could have delayed enrolling in Parts B and D. She had paid more than $10,000 in premiums, but her money is lost because the federal government does not refund premiums paid by mistake.

Contacting a Medicare-trained broker who can compare all the options in your service area can help prevent you from making costly mistakes like this. A broker can also do a comparative analysis between the employer retiree plan and available individual plans to guide you to get the best coverage for the least cost.

Question 10: *What are the penalties, if any, if I don't sign up for Medicare?*

Bonnie Dobbs:

The "gotcha" about Part B and D can be tricky to understand because they are thought to be voluntary. The truth is you must enroll and stay enrolled once you become Medicare eligible or incur a lifelong penalty unless you have credible coverage through another source, like employer coverage.

Part B and Part D have specified enrollment requirements. If you miss those deadlines, the Part B penalty is 10 percent of the Part B premium for each year you are not enrolled.

Part D penalty is one percent per month of the national average which for 2022 is about $35.00 per month and equates to approximately $0.35 a month for every month you are not enrolled.

Once a penalty has been accessed, it will apply for as long as you have Medicare.

Anytime you cancel enrollment in either Part B or Part D, Medicare has specifications about when you are eligible to enroll again.

Question 11: *Who can I contact if I don't have enough to pay Part B or medications? Will I pay more for Part B and Part D if I make high salary?*

Bonnie Dobbs:

Part B premium is based on income. Lower income individuals may be exempt, and Medicaid may pay. Medicaid is both a federal and state program that helps low-income individuals pay the Part B premium and lower the cost for medical services and medications. If paying Part B premium is impossible, contact the local Medicaid office or the plan with your concerns. Extra Help, also known as LIS (Low-Income Subsidy), is another program for individuals who cannot afford medications. There is a sliding scale with medications starting at $0 co-pay.

Higher income participants will pay a higher amount for both Part B and Part D. This is called IRMAA (Income Related Monthly Adjustment Amount). IRMAA has an escalating chart in increments up to over $750,000. There is a two-year look back. For example, in 2022, the cost is based on the MAGI (Modified Adjusted Gross Income) as reported on your 2020 tax return. If unsure where to find this information on your return, contact a CPA or tax advisor.

Question 12: *When can I change plans? What if I move?*

Bonnie Dobbs:

Annual enrollment period known as AEP is October 15 to December 7 each year. You can review and change Advantage or drug plans. All changes become effective January 1.

For those already on a plan, in September each year, you will receive an Annual Notice of Coverage booklet in the mail. This allows you to compare your current year plan, line item by line item, with the changes including costs for next year. If your doctors or medications have not changed, you can do nothing and let your plan roll over. However, if you did have some changes, or the costs for the next year has increased substantially, call a broker. Remember using a broker is no cost to you but can save you a lot of money.

Another time is OEP, also known as Open Enrollment Period, which is January 1 to March 31 each year. For Advantage plans only, if you are unhappy, you can change to another Advantage plan or prescription drug plan. If you medically qualify, you can add a Supplement plan. Understanding this qualifying factor is very important.

Another exception is to change plans, which is referred to as SEP (Special Election Periods). Some examples are moving into or out of a nursing home, qualifying or losing Medicaid, incarceration, and many more.

Important: If you move to a different state, county, or, yes, even if you move to a different county, please always have the plan reviewed. All plans are assigned to a specific service area. If you move out of your service area, you will be disenrolled and receive a lifelong penalty. Ugh! The good news is there may be better options in your new service area. Hurray!

Are there options available for you to access funds to help you in your retirement? Questions below can provide you some answers.

Question 13: *What resources are available for Veterans?*

Bonnie Dobbs:

A special pension, provided by the Department of Veterans Affairs, is a benefit for wartime veterans and their surviving spouse who need assistance by another person for at least two of the activities of daily living (ADL) like dressing, walking, eating, bathing, transferring, and the needs of nature.

The service eligibility requirements are: (1) you must have ninety days or more active wartime duty with at least one day during wartime, (2) been honorably or generally discharged, (3) be 65 years old or 100 percent disabled, and (4) you or your spouse must require independent, assisted living or home care.

If you serviced in any of the wars with the following dates, you qualify and should seek assistance:

- World War II: December 7, 1941 to December 31, 1946
- Korean: June 27, 1950 to January 31, 1955
- Vietnam: February 28, 1961 to August 4, 1964 (For veterans who served in the country, otherwise August 5, 1964 to May 7, 1975)
- Gulf War: August 20, 1990 to yet to be determined date

The amounts differ depending on your marital status. This money is tax free. At the time of publication, the allocations monthly are as follows:

• Two Married Veterans: $3,162
• Married Veterans: $2,431
• Single Veteran: $2,050
• Surviving Spouse of Veteran: $1,380

Some veterans do not think they qualify since the implementation of the new rules because of the look-back rule, the penalty period, and their net worth. Understanding, applying, and getting benefits can be complex. Talk to someone at the Veterans Benefits Administration or contact an elder care attorney that offers this service. An elder law attorney who specializes in VA benefits can help you file a claim at no charge. They can charge for any additional services.

Carmen Perry-Tevaga:

What is the Aid and Attendance Pension?
The Veterans Benefits Administration (VBA), a branch of the Department of Veterans Affairs (VA), offers tax-free, monthly monetary payments to certain wartime veterans with financial need and their survivors. The pension is a benefit for veterans who do not have a service-connected disability resulting from their military service.

VA Aid and Attendance is an additional monetary amount that can be added to the VA's pension. The enhanced Aid and Attendance amount is available for those who need the "aid and attendance" of another person for their routine daily living activities on a permanent basis.

It is widely known that the Veterans Benefits Administration offers disability compensation (tax-free funds) to veterans with disabilities that are the result of a disease or injury incurred or aggravated during active military service. However, many people are unaware that a VA Pension program exists for wartime veterans who do not have a service-connected disability.

One day of service during wartime is necessary for the VA Pension program, but the veteran does not need to have served in combat or overseas. Unlike the VA's Compensation program, veterans do not need to have a disability connected to their military service to be eligible for the VA Pension with Aid and Attendance.

A simple way to determine if you are eligible is to start with the three main qualifications or "must-haves" for the VA Pension with Aid and Attendance: 1. Military, 2. Medical and 3. Money.

A veteran or veteran's surviving spouse will need to meet the following criteria:

1. Military

Are you a veteran or the surviving spouse of a veteran who (1) served at least ninety days on active duty, (2) has at least one day during wartime, (3) with an honorable or general discharge? (Persian Gulf War veterans must have two years of active duty or the full period for which they were called for active duty.)

2. Medical

Do you have a non-service-connected medical condition causing you to need assistance with activities of daily living (ADLs)?

Activities of daily living are routine self-care activities that people tend do every day without needing assistance. There are six basic ADLs: eating, bathing, dressing, continence (using the toilet), mobility (transferring, walking), and grooming. Home care agencies provide aides who can assist those who need help with activities of daily living.

3. Money

Do you have a net worth at or less than $138,439? (A limit was established by Congress in December 2021. It increases slightly each year.) A primary residence and auto are not counted as part of net worth. Ongoing non-reimbursable medical and long-term care expenses may reduce your countable income.

To find out more information, I have provided additional resources in the Notes and Additional Resources at the end of the book.

Question 14: *I would like to remain in my home. I have heard about reverse mortgages. Can you provide some information about reverse mortgages?*

Sue Haviland:

You've no doubt heard about a reverse mortgage, a loan for older adult homeowners that seems to be steeped in myths and misunderstanding. Let's set the record straight - the definition is fairly simple and straightforward - a reverse mortgage converts home equity into liquidity. It's a loan against your home's equity - that's it. It truly is a mortgage in reverse. Instead of the borrower being obligated to make monthly principal and interest payments to the lender, the lender disburses funds to the borrower.

How this product has evolved and become a part of a holistic retirement planning discussion for older homeowners is quite the story. From its humble beginnings in 1961, when the first reverse mortgage was written, to the safe and sound products we have today, the loan continues to evolve.

How a Reverse Mortgage Works

A reverse mortgage (yes, it is a mortgage) allows a borrower to access a portion of the equity in their primary residence without the obligation of making monthly mortgage payments. The funds can be used for practically any purpose.

The borrower(s) retain title to the home, and no other assets are at risk. The interest and other fees, if applicable, accrue on the loan and no repayment is due until a maturity event occurs. An example of a maturity event is the last borrower permanently leaving the home. The non-recourse feature of the reverse mortgages of today protects the borrowers and the heirs, as they are not held liable for any deficit at the time the home is sold, should the loan balance be higher than the sales price. The borrower is responsible for the timely payment of all property charges. Some examples of these are real estate taxes, homeowner's insurance, and condo or HOA fees, if applicable.

Why Consider a Reverse Mortgage?

Why might someone consider the use of home equity in retirement? The short answer is many reasons. Some simply want to "retire" their current monthly principal and interest payments, giving them increased cash flow each month. Others seek to establish a secure line of credit for unforeseen expenses such as large medical bills. Still others look to satisfy long time goals like travel, helping grandchildren with college expenses, or even starting a new business. There are also those who may be looking for a way to pay for home modifications to complete their aging in place plan.

Maybe you know someone who has worked in his/her profession for many years and would love to retire, but that monthly mortgage payment is stopping them from realizing their dream of traveling around this beautiful country. Maybe you know someone who still loves what they do, but would rather volunteer their time versus having to work forty hours per week. Maybe you know someone who would like to access a lump sum of cash to purchase that vacation home they have wanted for years. Perhaps you know someone who loves his/her home but only uses a portion of it due to mobility issues; those steps to the second floor are difficult to navigate. Maybe you know someone - maybe it's you?

The Popular Type of Reverse Mortgage

The most popular type of reverse mortgage is the FHA insured HECM, or Home Equity Conversion Mortgage, which was first offered in 1989 under President Ronald Reagan. HECM borrowers must be at least sixty-two years of age. The program offers important safeguards, such as mandatory counseling, the non-recourse feature, and limitations on the amount of funds that can be taken in the first year. These and other safeguards help to make the HECM a sustainable solution for the borrower.

To date, over a million older adult homeowners have utilized a HECM. Funds from a home equity conversion mortgage can be accessed in a number of ways, depending on the borrowers' needs and goals: structured monthly payments, lump sum, or one of the most popular options - a secured line of credit. In 2009, the HECM for Purchase product was introduced. This made it possible for a borrower to utilize a HECM to purchase a primary residence, which might better be suited to their aging in place goals.

Proprietary Reverse Mortgages

There are also proprietary products available in many states, some for borrowers as young as age fifty-five. Proprietary products differ from a HECM in that they are overseen by the lenders who offer them and are not FHA-insured. Check with a lender for specific features, state availability, and any state-specific requirements regarding proprietary reverse mortgage products.

Is a Reverse Mortgage for Me?

The best way to learn if a reverse mortgage is right for you, or someone you know, is to speak with a reverse mortgage specialist. Ask your family, friends, and other trusted advisors if they can make an introduction. Be sure to ask questions since reverse mortgages, like any financial product, are not for everyone. They are intended to be a long-term solution, and anyone considering a reverse mortgage should fully understand the features as well as the costs and requirements.

Peter Klamkin:

Put simply, a reverse mortgage is a loan against the equity in your home. The key advantage over a traditional home equity loan is that the loan does not need to be paid back until the last borrower leaves the home.

A Home Equity Line of Credit requires a stricter set of qualification guidelines, must begin to be paid back immediately, and can be frozen. A reverse mortgage has qualifications which can be less strict, but doesn't need to be paid back immediately and cannot be frozen.

Reverse mortgages are not for everyone. First and foremost, if you are planning to leave your home within a year or so, given the costs involved with a reverse mortgage, it may not make sense to take one.

Why a Reverse Mortgage?

Started in 1989 under the Reagan administration, reverse mortgages were designed to help seniors age in place with easier access to their home equity. The premise was, and is, that as we age we have less opportunities to earn money. The older you are, the more money you may be able to access. At the qualifying age of sixty-two, you are still apt to work. At age ninety-two, chances are you are not going to be a greeter at Walmart. It is the opposite of life insurance where the older you are, the higher the premiums and benefit may be. Despite all of the advertising, education, movie star spokespersons, and press, no financial product has been more misunderstood than reverse mortgages. Part of it is the initial product itself, and the market it serves. Despite this, there is currently over $11 trillion in un-tapped equity in seniors' homes. There are over a million seniors who have taken a reverse mortgage, and more and more changes have been made to protect seniors. The biggest protection, as these are government-insured loans for the most part, is third-party, HUD-approved counseling.

No application can move forward without counseling. Older adults are encouraged to have those whom they rely on to be part of the counseling session. This could include children, financial advisors, attorneys, and others. Counseling protects the borrower(s), the loan originator, the lender, and advisors.

Another important protection is time. In most states, and depending on the product, borrowers have a three-day right of rescission, after the loan funds. In other words, you can still change your mind at the last minute. Again, some states such as California vary in length, but this is another important protection.

Reverse Mortgage - Where to Begin?

Start by asking your trusted advisors if they have a relationship with a local reverse mortgage specialist: most do. It is possible your friends and family may have taken a reverse mortgage. At one point, there was a stigma concerning reverse mortgages. However, over the years as more protections were put in place and using home equity has become accepted as part of a solid retirement plan, much of that has gone away.

Check online for reviews of companies. Generally, all reverse mortgage companies sell the same product, so particularly look for quality of service, fees which can be negotiated (such as origination fees) and most importantly - rates. You are free to shop, especially if you do not feel comfortable with the loan officer or the company.

Finally, there is one protection the government put in place which has helped. Most loans do not allow you to take all your loan proceeds at once. Before this change, funds could be distributed in a lump sum, which often was used too quickly. Reasons for use included: children looking to buy a home, grandchildren needed money for college, buying a car. Older adults found it difficult to say no and the money went fast. Make sure you know how your funds will be distributed and what options, such as being paid monthly, quarterly, or any combination, you may want.

Question 15: *What resources are available to assist low-income households?*

When locating resources for low-income households, you can feel as if you are searching for a needle in a haystack. Resources may seem to be available; but when you start diving deeper into eligibility and availability, you may become overwhelmed and discouraged.

It has been determined that older adults apply for low-income benefits at significantly lower rates than other demographics - even though there are greater out-of-pocket health care expenses. Whatever resources you are looking for, do not give up!

Numerous public and private programs may provide financial assistance to vulnerable older adults. However, a sizable proportion of eligible older adults do not participate in the programs. In some cases, as few as 25 percent of eligible participants apply for a program.

One recent study suggested that enrollment would increase by growing awareness of programs and simplifying the application process. I must agree that awareness is lacking, but the complicated applications are what deter most people.

When I meet clients with limited resources, but want to remain in their homes, I immediately reach out to my professional network to find what is available in the local region. If this is not your full-time career, and you do not have a network of industry professionals to lean on, then where do you turn?

Here are two resources I have found easy to use:

1. Benefits Checkup - www.BenefitsCheckUp.org

Benefitscheckup.org is a service developed and maintained by the National Council on Aging. The site is a comprehensive web-based service that matches benefits programs to older adults with limited income and resources. The site includes information on more than 1,700 public and private benefits programs, including benefits for: prescription drugs, nutrition, energy assistance, financial, legal, health care, Social Security, housing, in-home services, tax relief, transportation, educational assistance, employment, and volunteer services.

This user-friendly website has large print for the visually impaired and very easy links to use for the specific assistance you need.

2. Unite Us - www.uniteus.com/networks

Unite Us is a national platform that aligns stakeholders from healthcare, government, and the community around a shared goal to improve health. Their proven infrastructure provides both a person-centered care coordination platform and a hands-on community engagement process. They work together with communities to ensure services are seamlessly delivered to the people who need them most.

What is unique about the Unite Us platform is that it tracks outcomes. I do not know of any other program that makes sure each referral receives resolution to their inquiry for assistance. It is simple to use and once you enter your information into their system, it goes out to their resource partners to see how many organizations can get involved and provide appropriate assistance quickly.

These are both national platform resources, but do not discount the opportunities available in your own backyard. Every community has a local Senior Center. These centers always have a resource wall with information on community specific programs. The employees at these centers are also great guides to ask for help.

The underutilization of available programs is primarily driven by the lack of financial resources. If you find a resource for which you potentially qualify, make certain to ask for assistance in completing the application. You will often be required to submit income and asset verification with each application. Be sure to follow-up with the program once your application has been submitted to ensure it is in process.

Question 16: *What is the difference between a 401(k) plan and a pension?*

Peter Klamkin:

Not long ago working for a company meant having a defined benefit plan or pension as part of your employee package.

Over time, these employer contribution plans gave way to putting more of the burden on the employee by switching to 401(k) plans. Now, these plans are the norm. A pension plan might be a better fit for investors looking for a fixed income for life, while a 401(k) plan is better for those looking for more control over their retirement funds.

The big difference is a 401(k) is a defined contribution plan while a pension is a designed benefit plan.

As with other financial products, it is important to do two important things: (1) find an advisor you trust, and ask questions, and (2) do your research as your retirement and financial well-being depends on it.

Question 17: *What is involved with hospice care? Can hospice care be managed at home? Is there a cost?*

Fritzi Gros-Daillon, MS, CSA, CAPS, UDCP, SHSS:

Yes, hospice care can be managed at home. It is facilitated by hospice professionals; usually a registered nurse leads the hospice team for each client, and depending upon your region of the country, specific licensing may be required for each hospice organization. Hospice provides medical supervision for a patient whose end of life is expected within six months and offers caregiving respite and support to family members. The importance of hospice cannot be understated for individuals and families as an important care option.

I would like to share two stories for perspective from my personal experience. I was thirty-eight years old by the time my husband, who was fifty-one, had been in treatment for Hodgkin's lymphoma for five years. He had undergone surgery, several rounds of chemotherapy, and radiation procedures.

On a New Year's Eve, I drove him to the emergency room at New York's Memorial Sloan Kettering Hospital. His blood pressure was so low the physicians were stunned that he could still stand without assistance. Over the next four weeks, he endured countless tests, and we struggled to find, but ultimately located, a surgeon to perform a unique procedure to repair a hole in his diaphragm. The surgery lasted nine hours, requiring over twenty-five pints of blood to simply sustain him. In recovery, he was placed on a ventilator and the doctors advised me that it was unlikely he would survive the first night. Miraculously, he did. He lived for a few days more, and ultimately slipped away at 5:00 a.m. on January 30.

I share the details of this experience because I believe now, thirty-two years later, that my husband would much rather have preferred to discontinue the treatments and return home for a more peaceful transition with his family nearby. The treating physicians were singularly focused on "life-saving" measures. We were so caught up in the "trying to save him" mode that other options were never considered or discussed. Now, years later and decades wiser, I strongly encourage families to have the very difficult conversation with your family member to consider and define what they would like you to do and how they want you to handle life and death circumstances like these.

The conversations are hard. The fears - for everyone involved - are real. But we do those we love a regrettable disservice if we don't provide them with the opportunity to choose to have a calmer, less invasive, more personal transition. As a caregiver or family member, you should take it upon yourself to learn as much as you can about the hospice services in your area. Our lack of knowledge about this important option may lead to unnecessary suffering.

Recently, a good friend required hospice care at home. Her husband was her primary caregiver. Two adult children who lived close by provided support to the dad, as well. The hospice nurse case manager visited weekly or as needed. The hospice team, including volunteers who provided respite for the husband, was instrumental in her care. The hospice nurse gave the family a twelve-page document that described the process of care, common questions and procedures for end-of-life notifications. But even though the document sat on the kitchen table in plain view for days upon days, the husband and his children ignored the document as if it wasn't there. Such was the demonstration of the emotional denial in which they were living.

I discovered this during a visit one day. As difficult and understandable as their avoidance was, I insisted that I would not leave until the husband had read the document front-to-back. He did and that new understanding very naturally led the family into the conversation they had all avoided. The following week, when the end-of-life moment arrived, her husband had a plan that was aligned with her wishes and knew exactly how to handle the processes of death. Later, he thanked me for insisting that he prepare himself with the information and ultimately, the peace of mind to act in accordance with hospice instruction and his wife's wishes.

So, my advice is simple: Read through and understand the documents provided by the hospice team. Their goal is nothing more, or less, than detailing and simplifying the various aspects of hospice, home care, end-of-life procedures to give you, and those you love, greater peace of mind over the inevitable.

Question 18: *What should I do if I have not arranged for my funeral? Where do I start? What costs are involved? What happens if I don't have a lot of money to pay for my funeral?*

Peter Klamkin:

We plan for major life events such as birthdays, weddings, and anniversaries. But, when it comes to planning for funerals, little to nothing is usually done. This leaves the burden to loved ones, those who are going through one of the worst moments of their lives as it is. Funeral planning in advance creates peace of mind and the ability to meet your wishes and values, not to those who may have to guess what your wishes would be, or worse, impose what their wishes would be.

Over the years, the desire to plan funerals in advance has grown. It may be due to: (1) more acceptance and lessening the fear and stigma of planning a funeral, and (2) more marketing has been done, which has opened conversations within families as to what one's funeral could include.

Choices to Be Made

There are many choices to make, the biggest being burial or cremation. Cremation is generally considered to be less expensive, but the reality is cremation can cost as much as a burial, depending on the type of service. No matter the decisions which need to be made, the key is to begin by having a clear mind. Write down all the things which are important to you. There are many guides available to use as a format.

The best place to start is with your local funeral home. Most have specialists in pre-arranging funerals and can take you through your options. By law, they must provide you with a copy of their price list without hesitation. The Federal Trade Commission regulates this heavily and funeral homes must comply.

Facts to Consider

There are several keys to consider. First, you are free to shop. There is nothing to prevent you from going to different funeral homes in your area. Ask if they are corporate-owned or family-owned. It may be that they have served your family in the past, but with a more transient society this is getting to be a far less occurrence. A family-owned funeral home may not have the overhead of a corporate-owned and may be able to work with you on prices.

Once you have selected the type of service, the next step is to decide if you want to pay for it in advance. Paying in advance can and should mean the funeral home will lock or freeze charges they can control. Those are charges such as their service charge, embalming if desired, or required by law, casket if desired, and other in-house services.

Outside charges can include the cost of location, cemetery space, opening of the grave, and clergy. The funeral home will show you what can be guaranteed and what may not be. Every funeral home has file cabinets full of people who have decided to prearrange their funeral and never fund it. But there are options on funding and thus guaranteeing prices. The first is to pay the full amount which the funeral home can put in a trust account. The interest on a trust account may be taxable, which is an important question to ask.

The alternative is to ask if the funeral home uses an insurance policy as a funding vehicle. Most do. The advantage of an insurance policy is the growth is tax-free, and there are a variety of payment options while still guaranteeing the costs of goods and services. Again, no matter what, even if you don't have funds, it's important to let loved ones know what your wishes are and to have it in writing. This document should be kept with your other important papers and easily accessible at the time of need.

Options to Cover Financial Expense

There are financial resources which may be available to you depending on your situation. The first is whether you are a veteran. The Veterans Administration (VA) will pay for some of your costs, but not all. The VA will provide a burial allowance as a tax-free benefit but at an amount not likely to cover the full costs. They will provide a gravesite in any national cemetery at no charge, but many of these spaces fill quickly.

Some people assume that the Social Security Administration will cover funeral costs. The reality is the funeral benefit provided by Social Security is $255. It has not changed and is not likely to change anytime soon.

If neither of these options are a fit, especially if funds are an issue, you have at least two alternatives. The first is body donation, usually done in conjunction with a local medical school. Donating one's body to science has increasingly become a more recognized option.

Another option is a funeral provided by the state or county, depending on where you live. A "welfare" funeral benefit varies widely and your funeral director will know how to best proceed if this is the only option available.

At the least, the best place to start is to have a conversation with those near to you, and write down all the things you find important. Once the discussion starts, you and your loved ones will feel more comfortable with the conversation. You just have to start.

AREAS TO CONSIDER

1. Do you currently have sufficient income and/or savings to cover your monthly expenses?

2. Do you feel comfortable that you have enough money to get you through retirement?

3. Are you currently collecting Social Security benefits? If no, have you decided when you will start collecting your Social Security?

4. Have you considered Long-Term Care Insurance?

5. Have you completed the appropriate legal documents, including a financial power of attorney and a will, for the disposition of assets?

6. Have you made arrangements for your funeral? Is your family aware of your wishes?

For more Areas to Consider related to the Personal Finance Pillar, download the *Act III: Your Plan for Aging in Place* at https://naipc.memberclicks.net/ or scan the QR code:

Pillar 4: Transportation

 Human nature has a way of ignoring what it sees as routine. Driving a vehicle is one of those activities. Until you do not have the ability or option to drive a vehicle to stop by the store, visit family and friends, or even take a trip to the doctor for a check-up, you take for granted driving a car. What do you do if driving a car is no longer available to you?

If this is you, we actually have good news to share. There are many options available to you to get where you need to go, and you are not alone! Did you know that the market value for ride-sharing is estimated to reach $61.24 billion by the year 2026? Clearly, a lot of people are using this resource, and there are other choices available to you.

Whether you are open to ride-sharing services or want to choose another option, we are confident you will find the information in this chapter extremely helpful.

Question 1: *I worry about transportation to go to the doctor or the store. My family is not always available, and I'm afraid to use a ride-sharing service. What are my alternatives for transportation?*

Tara Ballman, MBA:
According to the *Aging Americans: Stranded Without Options Study*, "Over 1 in 5 adults over the age of 65 in the U.S. do not drive, and over half of these individuals stay

home...because they do not have transportation options." This study revealed the impact of the inability to drive on older adults: 15 percent make fewer doctor appointments, 60 percent take fewer shopping trips, and 65 percent visit friends, family, or religious gatherings less often than they would like.

People often overlook the transportation aspect of aging in place. An AARP study on transportation revealed that 78 percent of baby boomers see driving as their key to independence, but there are so many options in today's world if you are unable to continue driving yourself.

To ensure continued, reliable transportation as you age and your physical needs change, become familiar with the options in your neighborhood before there is a need. Often older adults rely on friends or family, and it ends up feeling like a burden for both parties. Let me share some of the options available to you for meeting your transportation needs.

Arranged Transportation and Shuttle Buses

Local senior centers and county/government organizations may provide fare assistance, low-cost, or no-cost rides for older adults who meet program eligibility requirements. Many of these programs take age, disability level, and/or income into consideration. This is generally door-to-door service to grocery stores, senior centers, medical offices, or other specified locations. These types of transportation usually can accommodate a wheelchair or other mobility device.

Some organizations also offer door-through-door service for those needing assistance getting in and out of the vehicle or walking into a building. In some cases, a personal care attendant or family member may be allowed to ride with the older adult.

Not all options may be available in your community, but there are regional organizations that can connect you with local options. Here's a few that can help:

1. Area Agency on Aging (AAA)

With over 600 AAAs across the U.S., this network of nonprofit agencies is supported by federal funds under the Older Americans Act. Be sure to ask for a mobility counselor familiar with transportation options in your area. If you are unsure of how to connect with your local AAA, contact the Eldercare Call Center at (800) 677-1116 or chat online at eldercare.acl.gov.

2. Centers for Independent Living (CIL)

The Centers for Independent Living are a part of the Administration for Community Living (ACL). This program is designed and operated by others with disabilities and promotes independent living programs. For a list of resources available for transportation and other areas, visit https://acl.gov/programs/aging-and-disability-networks.

3. Aging and Disability Resource Centers (ADRCs)

This is another organization that works through the Administration for Community Living (ACL) to provide long-term services to older adults and their families. ADRCs' work in partnership with Centers for Medicare & Medicaid and the Veterans Health Administration and offer unbiased information and counseling, regardless of income.

4. National Aging and Disability Transportation Center (NADTC)

NADTC's mission "promotes the availability and accessibility of transportation options for older adults, people with disabilities, and caregivers." For more information on the options available through this organization, contact (866) 983-3222 or visit https://www.nadtc.org/about/contact-us/.

On-Demand and Shared-Ride Services

Most taxi companies have some type of accessible vehicle in their fleets. Some community agencies offer vouchers to older adults who meet certain eligibility requirements. This is information that your local AAA can provide.

The idea of using Lyft or Uber can be daunting, especially when smartphones and apps are involved. But concierge services that can help make the process more comfortable are popping up. It is not necessary to pre-schedule rides, which are available all day, every day. A car can typically be at your location within minutes of calling - depending on the time and day - using a regular touchtone phone.

These curb-to-curb services are great for older adults who don't need mobility assistance, and they will make accommodations for walkers and foldable wheelchairs. The service also provides friends or family with text notifications of your progress.

Ride-share fares are usually lower than taxi rates, but an additional fee is charged for the on-demand services. For example, GoGoGrandparent (https://gogograndparent.com) is a concierge service that offers subscription-based plans, starting around $8.00 per month. Its premium and "total care" packages can include unlimited operator-ordered rides, meal delivery, grocery delivery, pharmacy services, home services (e.g., connections with lawn services, housekeepers, etc.), priority support, and proactive care management.

Older adults who use Jitterbug phones (cell phones designed specifically for older users) can hit "0" and tell their personal operator where they would like to go. The caller will be given an estimated arrival time and cost, and the charge for the ride will automatically be included in the next phone bill.

Ride-sharing organizations have recently begun partnering with organizations servicing older adults. Lyft is one of the more popular on-demand ride-share companies, and it is establishing partnerships with assisted living communities and health organizations. If you become more comfortable using smartphone apps and can get in and out of a vehicle without assistance, this would be a viable option. Bring a friend if you aren't comfortable riding alone. The cost is generally less than a taxi, and you'll have a car at your location within minutes.

Fixed Public Transportation Routes and Paratransit

You can search for local bus and rail routes many ways, but an easy way to navigate public transportation is through Google Maps. You can download the app onto a smartphone or visit the website. After you enter your destination and hit directions, you can adjust the mode of transportation from car to public transportation - or even walking. Google will bring up all available public transit options and times.

Travel Tip: Before purchasing your tickets, inquire about half fare options available to Medicare cardholders who use public transportation during non-peak hours.

Many public transit agencies offer free travel training to help new riders become comfortable on public transit and learn how to safely navigate their route. In Orange County, California, the Orange County Transportation Authority (OCTA) offers online and in-person training in English, Spanish, Vietnamese, Korean, and Mandarin. The training covers everything from how to safely board and exit a bus to how to plan a trip. Classes are offered to individuals, as well as small and large groups and include two free one-day passes when the training is completed.

Public transportation may also offer special fixed routes for trips to and from a senior center. Call your local transit authority's call center to ask if there are any fixed route options available to older adults. In some cases, you may be able to complete a Reasonable Modification/ Accommodation Form to accommodate your specific situation.

The Americans with Disabilities Act (ADA) requires public transit agencies to offer paratransit services to those who are unable to use fixed bus or rail services. This is a door-to-door service and is available during the same working hours as other public transit.

Volunteer Transportation Programs

Your local AAA can help locate local nonprofit and faith-based organizations that have volunteer transportation programs. These rides are generally in an individual's private car - or sometimes an agency-owned vehicle - and can range from free to a small fee.

The Community Transportation Association of America (CTAA) is a nonprofit group in all 50 states, which provides rides to life-sustaining activities, ranging from medical visits to other necessary activities. These volunteers may offer door-to-door or door-through-door assistance, depending on the organization. You can find out more about its National Volunteer Transportation Center at https://ctaa.org/health-care-and-transportation/.

Other Options

Medicaid Non-Emergency Medical Transportation (NEMT) is an important benefit for people who do not have a driver's license or the ability to travel to and from medical appointments. Eligibility varies by situation, need, and state, and only covers you and an eligible family member to ride to and from medical offices.

For more information on this program, visit https://www.cms.gov/Medicare-Medicaid-Coordination/Fraud-Prevention/Medicaid-Integrity-Program/Education/Non-Emergency-Medical-Transport.

There are also companies, like Veyo (https://veyo.com), that have partnered with insurance companies and healthcare organizations to provide non-emergency medical transportation for insurance subscribers. Veyo provides transportation to and from doctor's appointments and can accommodate everything from wheelchairs to stretchers. If you are part of a Medicare Advantage plan or Medicare HMO, ask if transportation is a plan benefit.

Question 2: *What is the best way to approach a loved one when it is time for them to stop driving?*

Tara Ballman, MBA:

No one wants to have a difficult conversation about "taking away" the car keys, but according to 2019 data by the Centers for Disease Control and Prevention (CDC), more than twenty older adults are killed and approximately 700 are injured in accidents each day. Start talking about alternatives to driving before it becomes a crisis. The conversation will be less awkward and argumentative if you have already discussed the subject - even better if you have alternatives to provide.

Driving does not have to be all-or-nothing. Adjustment can be made based on your loved one's situation. Regular eye exams and health check-ups are an important part of the process. Making small adjustments are perfectly acceptable, like not driving at night or on the highways during rush hour. There may also be underlying medical issues that can be addressed before driving can become safe again. Examples include: (1) cataract surgery to regain safe eyesight for driving, or (2) controlling diabetes to address blood sugar levels that may suddenly dip.

There are red flags of which families should be aware. But everyone's situation will be different and should not be compared with a friend who did this or when a neighbor did that. Here are a few things to look out for:

• A medical diagnosis. Examples include dementia, epilepsy, glaucoma, etc.
• Fresh dents and dings on the vehicle.
• A change in their driving behavior: straining to see, running red lights and stop signs, or stopping at green lights, driving extremely slowly.
• A general loss of strength or stiffness in the neck or legs that can hinder driving ability.

There are many organizations, such as AARP's Driver Safety program (www.aarp.org/auto/driver-safety), that can help you evaluate and provide recommendations and/or refresher courses. If you are looking for a safe driving program in your area, visit the directory at www.ageinplace.org or call your local AAA office. (See Question #1 above for additional information on AAA.)

Many automobiles have add-on features that assist in safer driving. You may want to research the items different car brands consider "standard" safety features including blind spot awareness to back-up cameras and voice-activated controls. Depending on the vehicle and safety features, the add-ons can be pricey, but many now come standard.

If all else fails, it is possible for you to anonymously report your loved one to the Department of Motor Vehicles (DMV). Most people believe that a doctor must complete the report, but anyone can file the paperwork. Although each state is different, the driver will be called in for a driving test, and the DMV will make the determination.

Additional resources and links are provided in the Notes and Additional Resources chapter.

AREAS TO CONSIDER

1. Do you live in a(n):
• Urban community
• Suburban community
• Rural community

2. What is the most common form of transportation in your community?
• Car
• Walking
• Bus
• Train
• Taxi
• Uber/Lyft

3. If driving a car is the most common form of transportation, are you still able to drive safely and comfortably?
• If you answered "yes," do you have a plan in place for your future transportation needs if your ability to drive changes?
• If you answered "no," do you have family or friends who can assist you with your transportation needs?
• If you answered "no," do you have access to public transportation?
• If you answered "no," do you have access and the financial resources to cover a car service or ride sharing service?
• If you answered "no," do you have access to programs through local non-profits like the Village to Village Network or volunteer services?

For more Areas to Consider related to the Transportation Pillar, download the *Act III: Your Plan for Aging in Place* at https://naipc.memberclicks.net/ or scan the QR code:

Pillar 5: Community and Social Interaction

 Remaining socially engaged and discovering ways to be part of your different communities is the key to better aging in place. Maintaining a healthy social interaction with others is what can lighten your mood, mitigate feeling depressed, and ultimately promote a sense of well-being, feeling safe, and secure.

What does being socially engaged and a part of your community look like? It is a question only you can answer. You may decide that continuing to work may be the answer. Maybe now is the time to pursue a hobby, participate as a community volunteer, or even learn new ways of interacting with a computer if you are spending more time at home. The exciting thing is there is no wrong answer. This may be the door of opportunity opening to discover new aspects and interests that will be fun and motivating. Just walk through the door.

We believe the authors in this chapter will open up some intriguing insights on the topic of community and social interaction. Look at Pillar 5 as a new adventure.

Question 1: *When I grew up, the retirement age was 65. However, I don't see myself retiring any time soon because I'm still able and want to work. Has this expectation in society changed?*

Fritzi Gros-Daillon, MS, CSA, CAPS, UDCP, SHSS:

Yes, there is evidence of this societal shift toward postponing retirement described in a major new study conducted by *National Geographic* magazine and AARP in late 2021, post-COVID-19. Most significantly, one's retirement age is no longer mandated in most professions. Today, the decision to retire is almost entirely based on your individual circumstances.

For many, the driving influence on when to retire is financial. Financial advisors have reported that the boomer generation is largely unprepared for retirement as a result of their savings and spending patterns over the many decades of their work life. A realistic look at your financial and fiscal plan is a vital step before you retire, preferably several years before you even consider a possible retirement date.

For many, an equal imperative when considering retirement is the contribution that work brings to your life and the value you glean from your role in a company, business, or organization, whether working for someone else or self-employed. The practical and intrinsic advantages of involvement cannot be understated. When we feel that we are an important part of a team (as leaders, managers, employees), that sense of participation supports our sense of well-being and our continued desire to work.

Interestingly, the *National Geographic-AARP* study found that of the 50 percent of those who believed that they would keep working past age sixty-five, the majority had changed their minds and retired early due to the pandemic. Influencing their decision was the prevailing belief that they could find a different/better job with greater flexibility, more opportunity for growth, better pay and benefits than the ones they were leaving. The creation of an encore career has blossomed in recent years with people leaving positions to find or create businesses with more flexibility in line with their interests and passions.

Of yet another group of surveyed individuals over the age of eighty who did not retire until after the age of seventy, 3 percent of them are still working. The desire to keep working, earning, and contributing is part of their personal decision and social changes seem to be supporting their decision to continue. This is the same criteria for you - make your decision based upon your circumstances, take into account all arenas of your life - financial, personal, health, and social. In this way, societal norms or pressures will not influence the steps you take toward your own future.

Ryan McEniff:

At what age someone retires is highly dependent on multiple factors, but many people will work well into their 70s. Over the last two presidential elections, we had many candidates who were well in their late sixties and early seventies vying for the nation's top job. If there is a stigma with working past a certain age, it is quickly vanishing.

For many, retirement is still fruitful. Someone has left their primary career to enjoy doing something they are more passionate about while still earning income. If you enjoy what you do, why would you stop? I believe people need a reason to get up in the morning.

Additionally, many people need to work because of money. COVID-19 has thrown many people, both young and old, into uncertain waters. People are unsure about the future and are concerned that saving more might be needed to weather future storms.

Any stigma of retiring at a certain age because of pensions or mandatory retirement is gone. Companies want to hire talented people who are capable of performing at a high level. People do not have the time to be worried about what you are doing. They are generally too focused on their own lives, family, and career. Work for as long as you like!

Steve Toll, BS, QDCS:

What do you want to be when you grow up? I can remember being asked this question countless times when I was a young boy, and I always had a different answer based on whatever I was curious about on that day. There was always something that could capture my attention, and I would dream about being all grown up and how much I looked forward to it.

Through my life, I have often thought about my early years and am always amazed about the twists and turns that life inevitably offers. For me, there has always been that constant curiosity. Although I feel the aging in my body, my spirit still feels youthful. The concept of retirement seems obscure and incomprehensible. I still have the desire to work and stay connected to other people. I have always loved the synergy of teams and the creative process.

Retirement is a personal decision and whatever society has to say about it is irrelevant. If you are ready to retire at age sixty-five, go for it. But, if you are like me and want to keep working, that is fine, too. The most important consideration is finding a way to stay socially connected; for many of us the solution is to keep working for as long as possible. Keep dreaming and remain curious about all the amazing things that the world has to offer, because we never stop growing up.

Question 2: *I have remained updated about technology. How much do I need to know to manage my personal and work life?*

Fritzi Gros-Daillon, MS, CSA, CAPS, UDCP, SHSS:

Keeping updated with technology can be daunting and to acknowledge that you feel current is a credit to you! We each manage technology in varying degrees, but essentially technology is designed to simplify and streamline the tasks of living. The bottom line is that technology presents options in almost every aspect of our lives.

For example, a simple grocery list can be prepared in at least three ways: handwritten, dictated into a note-taking app on a smartphone, or created with a voice-activated system, such as Amazon Alexa or Google Home. But then, when you go to the grocery store, which list do you take? Did you clip the paper coupons from the weekly flyer or clip the digital coupons in the grocery store app? Or perhaps you utilized technology to order your groceries from a local or national company to have them delivered to your home. This is just one of the myriads of tasks in our everyday lives that can be facilitated by technology.

In our homes, technology is impacting systems for lighting, heating, cooling and security and how we control them. Think about how much easier and more effective and reliable it is to save energy and reduce the utility bill because technology systems allow us to set temperatures based on our lifestyle. Advanced developments in voice and motion-activated doorbells, lights, and door locks with digital entry have vastly improved our security and safety.

Technology improvements in personal emergency response systems and telehealth monitoring continue to save thousands of lives every year-lives that might have been lost before technology tools became commonplace. These and other similar medical/telehealth advancements help us receive vital health care support, for example, as with virtual appointments. Chronic conditions like diabetes (with an external arm patch monitor sending data to a smartphone application) are now much more effectively monitored and controlled with technology. We couldn't have even imagined these devices two decades ago.

Keeping up with technology applications can improve our access to transportation with ride-sharing services to facilitate secure rides to appointments or shopping. They can also expand our arena for fun, engagement, and pleasure. Of course, we are aware of the social impact of services like Facebook or Twitter-platforms that have facilitated our connection to others and broadened our social circle. While the necessity brought on by COVID-19 for virtual social gatherings has lessened, there is a residual component that will remain embedded in our way of life. Zoom is now far less intimidating than it used to be and has, for many of us, become an easy, effortless way of staying in touch in lieu of sometimes arduous travel requirements.

The use of technology in the past few years for our work and socializing has become a vital part of our lives. The proliferation of home offices, flex hours, and hybrid work environments are directly related to the increased use of technology. Staying current on the use of communication technology is important to be able to contribute and conduct our work.

The necessity to learn a variety of platforms and tools will vary with your work requirements. Sometimes the use of Zoom, for example, is enough; however, familiarity with other platforms, such as Microsoft or Google teams, will ensure that you can participate.

Ryan McEniff:

Technology can move quickly, but if you have remained updated about tech, you are in a great position. Understanding smartphones, email software, messaging applications, and business-focused software like Google Workspace or Microsoft Office allows you to be involved in whatever the latest trends are.

Fundamentally, there is no reason why people of any age can't learn something new. It all comes down to the individual's mindset and how focused they are to learn the latest app.

If you understand how to use a smartphone, any other questions can be answered on Reddit or Google search. There are amazing tech-focused YouTube channels that share news and review the latest products each week.

With the wealth of experience you already have, you shouldn't need to dedicate a lot of time each week to keep up with the latest improvements or new technologies that come out, especially if you are in a specific industry. Find the websites or YouTube channels that report on your industry improvements and updates. You will stay on top of things without much effort.

Steve Toll, BS, QDCS:

Life can feel like a rollercoaster sometimes, especially when it comes to staying abreast of the latest updates in the world of technology. Even so, most people can get up to speed and simplify many of the Instrumental Activities of Daily Living

(IADLs) with some easy-to-use technology techniques and skills. When it comes to hardware, most laptops, tablets, and smartphones will do everything you want without spending a fortune on your device. Check the reviews and watch some videos about the devices on YouTube.

Below are some ideas of how you can use technology:

1. Communication
Google is great for free email accounts and countless other applications like Google Drive for storing and sharing files, videos, and pictures.
  a) Text messaging on your phone keeps us connected.
  b) Video calls are simple with applications like Zoom and Google Meet.

2. Organization
Google's calendar syncs up with your email and gives you reminders for appointments and medication schedules.

3. Banking and Bill Paying
Once you get set up with online banking, it becomes a seamless process for keeping track of your finances and paying bills without the need for writing checks and sending them through the mail.

4. Current Events, Interests and Socialization
  a) Online newspaper and magazine subscriptions are available through Amazon and Google.
  b) Social media like Facebook, Instagram, LinkedIn, and YouTube keep us up-to-date with friends, family, and favorite organizations.

c) There are numerous online courses and information on any topic imaginable. A great place to start is searching on Google and YouTube

Keep it simple. Ask questions and have fun. The world of technology can be a great source of joy. The old saying that *you can't teach an old dog new tricks* is a complete fabrication. Learning new things keeps our minds and spirits youthful and active.

Question 3: *I work with young people and want to be a better communicator with them. How do I stay relevant so I don't sound like an "old" person?*

Fritzi Gros-Daillon, MS, CSA, CAPS, UDCP, SHSS:

To answer the above question, I shared it with young people born into the millennial generation who are working in a corporate environment. I shared a bit of my own perspective when I posed the question to them. The following is their answer with some very succinct wisdom:

"Acknowledge your own wisdom; remember to just be you. Don't focus on 'being old' but the wisdom that age provides. You treat them as people and engage in active listening, acknowledge anything that is relatable, and lead by example in conversation 101. Ask leading questions, and even if you don't understand all of the specifics of the answer, chances are your young person or persons won't leave you hanging. An older person has more experience and immediate authority and respect. Be an active listener and find a way to insert yourself into the conversation. Take the leap, old people, and listen up, young people."

There you have it: sage advice. Often as the "old" person in the room, we are intimidated by the knowledge and perceived skills that we see in others. Sometimes, we are daunted by the sheer speed at which some people talk or communicate electronically. The astute advice from these young people is to not underestimate ourselves and recognize our knowledge, creativity, problem-solving skills, and resiliency. Be a positive contributor by utilizing good listening skills to find the collaborative language to enhance working relationships. Don't be afraid to ask questions, too, and participate! Don't shy away from learning or being the person from whom others can learn.

We bring who we are to the workplace as to all the other parts of our lives - volunteer work, community projects, and family gatherings. Trying to fit into a perceived persona is not only difficult and uncomfortable but can be counterproductive, especially in the workplace.

Ryan McEniff:

If you are thirty or more years older than the person you are talking with, they are not going to consider you "young"! But do not worry; it is probably easier than you think to be relatable and trusted.

Communication with younger people should start with focusing on what the latest trends are, which make it easier to relate. This could involve celebrities, fashion, slang, dance, film, and music. Today it is easier than ever to stay current and connected with the latest trends and fads. Social media allows you to take a few minutes a week to see what is happening in the world of pop culture.

We all go through similar experiences and growing pains in life include first loves, professional mistakes, and life's lessons. Sharing your life experiences will open the opportunity for them to share their current situation. Let them know about your challenges and mistakes. It shows that you are not perfect and have likely experienced what they are going through. Being honest about your struggles opens the door through which they can come to you to problem-solve an issue, get advice, or just talk.

Question 4: *How do I stay socially connected to the people in my life circle (i.e., family, friends, community, doctors, or house of worship)?*

Amy Miller:

Be intentional in how you want to stay engaged. I learned this lesson from an 85-year young man, Dave, who shared this nugget with me: commit to making three people smile or laugh every day. As a result, Dave has his days filled with joy and mirth. Dave started to live with this intention after he lost his beloved wife. While he misses his wife, this simple act provides him a personal purpose for each day.

Regarding technology, older adults have been learning to use their cell phones to connect to the internet and do video conferencing. In the past few years, many older adults have learned how to make video calls to their doctors and attend family gatherings with loved ones from around the U.S. or the world. Others are doing their banking and shopping online. Many remain wary of wearable devices, but they know it can bring peace of mind to their loved ones.

Pets provide a great outlet for many older adults. Receiving affection and having responsibility to provide for them is a wonderful outlet for many who are isolated in their homes. This gives a reason to go for a walk or go shopping to get them food and treats. For some older adults that cannot have a live pet due to dementia or allergies, benefit from having a companion pet like those provided by Ageless Joy. These toys offer many of the same needs of a live pet such as purring when being petted or barking for attention. The best part is they do not need to be cleaned up or fed.

One thing most retirees look forward to after leaving their careers is to share their life experience and wisdom through volunteering. Communities have local programs through their places of worship, community education, or school programs to help with a reading program, homework help or as a playground monitor. National programs with local offices such as Volunteers in Action and AARP which are designed for those who want to give back. Many professionals will share their knowledge and skill by volunteering with SCORE to help small business owners launch a new business.

See the Notes and Additional Resources chapter at the end of this book for links to the websites I mentioned and information about my free weekly online video conference meeting for older adults.

Steve Toll, BS, QDCS:

There is lots of buzz these days about the importance of staying socially connected. Sometimes I feel that this calling has become very stressful for many people. Of course, cutting ourselves off from society is probably not a great idea, but just how much social connection we need is a personal decision. The important distinction that needs to be made is the difference between social isolation and loneliness.

Of course, we all feel lonely from time to time, especially after life events like losing someone close or becoming an empty nester. These are all aspects of aging that are part of the human experience. Chronic loneliness is something else entirely. In adults, loneliness can be a major cause of depression, substance abuse problems, and is increasingly linked to a range of medical problems. Loneliness raises levels of circulating stress hormones and blood pressure. It undermines regulation of the circulatory system so that the heart muscle works harder.

People who are lonely also can become unable to detect a positive social interaction and may feel threatened. Sleep problems and the inability to relax may also occur from loneliness. All of these indicators for the need to feel socially connected can be achieved without the need to make major adjustments to your life. In fact, sometimes a simple attitude adjustment and how you perceive yourself as part of society is all that is needed.

For many people, being alone with the activities, hobbies, and interests they enjoy offers contentment. At the later stages of life getting used to more quiet time can be comforting. However, the challenge is finding that sweet spot between your alone time, social time, and how much time is needed to feel connected to society. Sometimes just a simple smile and greeting with a neighbor may be all that is needed. Even a short interaction with the person who delivers your groceries can make you feel connected. Chatting on the phone or having a video call with a friend or family member can get you through the day feeling connected. For others, getting out of the house may pose problems, but inviting someone over for a cup of tea or coffee can be very satisfying.

If you are longing for connection, there are many options available in this modern world filled with amazing technology. Interacting with others using video is a great alternative and can make you feel like you are really there. Applications like FaceTime, WhatsApp, Zoom, and Skype let you make a video call on your phone or computer in minutes. Seeing someone's face and smiling eyes can give you that warm connected feeling. Use these apps to connect with friends and family every day and remind yourself and them that you are not alone. You can even watch a movie together with friends and family using applications like Netflix Party. This application lets you synchronize your video and talk while watching together through a group chat.

Social media platforms are great for keeping up with friends and family as well as organizations you may be interested in. The "Live" feature of both Facebook and Instagram is an enjoyable and fun way to watch live-streamed videos from friends and organizations you follow. You can also communicate with medical professionals through online visits. If you are not familiar with how to use these applications, there are many free tutorials and resources to help you learn available on YouTube.

Remember to have fun and keep a positive attitude. At the end of the day, the friendly and loving connection with yourself is the most important connection to have.

Question 5: *I recently lost my spouse. It seems like all my friends are passing away. I'm feeling lonelier than ever before in my life. What is the best way to deal with bereavement?*

Deanne O'Rear Cameron:

Experiencing loss of a spouse can be a very deep-rooted pain. This is someone you built a life together with, filled with many memories and love. When you add friends who are transitioning as well, you feel lost and lonely.

Giving yourself the space and time to go through the stages of grief is important (denial, anger, bargaining, depression, and acceptance). You may go through them in different stages and hop between them, which is okay. Grief looks different for everyone as we are all unique and so are our relationships. Understanding that these stages are a part of the process and not judging yourself as you go through them is best. Many times, when working through loss, we almost feel it's necessary to be sad and not move on too quickly. This is because we feel we are dishonoring our loved one or ourselves when in fact, we are not. The best thing we can do is ask ourselves if they want me to feel this way. I'm quite sure the answer would be no. They would just want you to remember them with love, joy, and beautiful memories that will last a lifetime.

To find and talk with people who are impartial and has gone through the grieving process themselves can be beneficial. There are also people you can reach out to such as grief counselors, clergy at churches, and other support organizations. Not only can they assist with how you are feeling, many have activities or groups that will help with loneliness, keep your mind busy, and the opportunity to make new friends.

If you are not careful, too much time to think can be your enemy. Our thoughts at the time of loss and loneliness can sometimes lead us into a very negative place. This is not an experience our spouse, loved ones, or friends would ever want us to be in. I found through my own losses that taking the time to go through the good memories like photographs allows you to reflect and realize how lucky you were to have that person in your life. It sincerely helps.

Focus on all the good you experienced rather than the loss. It will always help the healing process. What we focus on expands, so focus on the good. No one can take those memories away; they are yours forever. Another way to heal may be to speak with others who knew the person who has passed and share memories together. It can be fun to learn more about your loved one or friend in the process, too. You may even find yourself laughing at some of the memories, and as they say, laughter is the best medicine.

Get involved in your favorite hobbies or find new ones is also another way to help your mind through the process. Staying active is not only good for the body, it is important for the mind. Maybe find out if a community center has offerings that interest you. Can they help with a hobby or introduce you to new people? It will help you get moving forward in your new reality of living without your loved one or friend. At first, you may not want to accept the words new reality. Yet, in time, you will come to understand they will always be with you, just in a different way.

Fritzi Gros-Daillon, MS, CSA, CAPS, UDCP, SHSS:

First, the idea that we grieve for a year and then move on magically when the twelve months end is old-school and out-of-date. Please give yourself permission to grieve in your own way and for as long as you feel the need to do so. Each of us individually needs to honor our grief and lean on the solace of our own routines. If you belong to a faith-based organization, you may find a bereavement support group there. Now that we can meet in-person more frequently, meetings like this are re-emerging and becoming, once again, a valuable resource for sharing, finding support, and even making new acquaintances and friends.

You may belong to other organizations that provide activities or missions that are still important to you. I would encourage you to continue to participate in roles you've already embraced and even consider expanding and offering more of your expertise, time or efforts to the group or organization. This may also be a good time to try something new or participate with a group whose interests have piqued your own. You might want to consider intergenerational programs-your local elementary school may need readers in the kindergarten classrooms. The local YMCA has music or art programs, and you may have a talent to share. You can conduct online research to identify nonprofit organizations and be blown away by the endless possibilities. Whether it is something you've been interested in for a long time or something brand new, grab your sense of adventure and give it a try. It is never easy to step into new groups, and sometimes bereavement can render this even more difficult. The first step will be the most difficult, but even if you start with just one thing, it will become easier over time.

With the passing of your spouse, you may find that your relationships with existing friends noticeably change. It is not uncommon to suddenly find yourself excluded from activities in which you used to be naturally included. You may feel resentful, outraged, neglected, offended, ostracized-new emotions compounded on top of the grief you're already experiencing. Please know that, unfortunately, this experience happens more often than not. It is generally not a reflection on you or the relationship that friends and family have with you individually. More often, it is a reaction by others to their sense of loss and grief and not knowing the appropriate way to include you. You're likely to find others through bereavement support groups, mentioned earlier, who are having the exact same experience.

Ultimately, the responsibility for combating our loneliness is in our own hands. It is hard and there are days when it is easier to simply feel the loneliness rather than take the steps to meet new people, call old friends, chat with the neighbors, or reach out to other family members. But the road to moving through grief and feeling happy again requires us to take the actions, small steps at a time.

Ronnie Genser:

First, let me extend my deepest sympathies to you. I would like to tell you about myself, so you know you are not alone. Then, I will share with you how I dealt with my own loss and the bereavement following the unexpected death of my beloved spouse from complications of a massive heart attack. Perhaps my experience can help you as you go through your journey.

We met in our early forties and married in our early fifties. He had been divorced; I had never been married. As a result, at the time of my marriage, I affectionately called myself "a first-time, albeit menopausal, bride." At the time of his death, he was sixty-one and I was sixty-three. It was a great ten-year marriage for which I feel truly blessed. However, my expectation for our relationship was always that "we would grow old together."

With his passing, there were so many activities that required my attention. In addition to the financial and non-financial parts of his estate, I had to notify family, friends, work associates, and close out all his work and volunteer activities. I found myself crying at some point every day from the grief, fatigue, and feeling overwhelmed. However, about a year and a half after his death, I started to feel slightly better. I began to ask myself "why?" as well as "will I feel better in time?" as other widows kept telling me I would. However, for a long time, I didn't believe them.

During this reemergence period, I found myself doing two things which really changed my narrative:

Attended a Grief Support Group

For eleven months, I attended a twice a month Sunday afternoon grief support group at a local in-patient hospice that was open to anyone. I had no idea why I decided to go, except it seemed to me like a "rite of passage" of something that I should do. Surprisingly, I met other widows and widowers who were about my age. It was one of the best things I did during this time!

Communities Become a Part of My Life

Along my journey, I began to view my life as a balanced three-legged wooden stool. Each of the legs of the stool represented one community that was, or had now become, part of my life.

Work Community
My work community included my business relationships, prospects, customers, and industry networking friends.

Faith Community
My faith community is my synagogue friends. In 2003, my husband and I were part of the founding members of Congregation Or Hadash, a conservative synagogue in Sandy Springs, Georgia, where we regularly attended Friday night services. After my husband died, I made a conscious decision to continue attending Friday night services. It had been a part of my weekly routine, and where I saw and interacted with friends on a regular basis.

Volunteer Community
My volunteer community is where I had my volunteer friends. I became a member of Assistance League - Atlanta, a chapter of a national all volunteer, nonprofit organization. This chapter is comprised of 250 retired women and some men, although a few members, like myself, still work.

What we have in common is we are all focused on giving back to the community, such as working in the chapter's thrift store called Attic Treasures in Chamblee, Georgia. One hundred percent of the thrift store proceeds help children and adults in need rebuild their lives and become more self-sufficient. Through the chapter's philanthropic programs and network of 250 community partners, the chapter provides new clothing, food, household goods, hygiene kits, comfort items, and educational aid to those affected by homelessness, abuse, and poverty.

Assistance League members are an exciting, vivacious, and energetic group of people. Everyone is always open to meeting new people. It has been a place where people didn't know me before the death of my husband. I made new friends, and it's where I always feel welcomed and valued. To find a chapter in your area, go to www.assistanceleague.org/find-a-chapter-or-thrift-shop-2.

I discovered in my journey that there are wonderful groups and communities that can give your life purpose and connection to people who can bring new joy to your life.

Peter Klamkin:

There is no easy answer when it comes to bereavement. Every situation is different as is every person. There is no "normal." You will be told what you're going through is to be expected; the question is, expected by whom? There is not one person who can honestly say, "They know what you're going through." They don't.

What is most important is to recognize you are not alone. Some days are worse than others, but again, there are resources available to help get through different stages of grief and loneliness. You may have friends and relatives who have lost someone near to them and have found ways to work through this. Ask them. Your funeral director or planning specialist will have lists of programs available to you. They may have their own program. They may also be aware of community outreach, especially through senior centers and programs through churches, synagogues, etc.

Recognize there will be times which can be worse than others. Holidays, birthdays, anniversaries, and other special moments will be difficult. While these can be your enemy, time is your friend. Your sense of loss and memories will never completely go away. But, with time, support, and new opportunities come a renewed sense of excitement, happiness, and perhaps love.

Most of us know of friends, relatives, and acquaintances who have thrived over time. They joined support groups, started new hobbies, traveled, moved to be closer to their children and grandchildren. One thing may not solve where you are in terms of a sense of loss and unhappiness, but combined it may make a difference.

My sister lost her husband when he was sixty-six and she was sixty-four. While her loss was devastating, several things helped her over time. She sold her business; she joined several book clubs, spends more time with her grandchildren, began art classes, designs and prints her own greeting cards, and travels.

On gray and rainy days, she makes a particular point to call her friends who have also lost their spouses and invites them to lunch. My sister knows she's not alone; she has a support group in her friends and family who care and love her.

You may not have an interest in working, but there are many ways to feel a sense of value, worth, and accomplishment. An important way is to volunteer. Ask others if they know programs and organizations looking for help. Volunteer where you might have a particular interest. Do you love animals? Volunteer at your local pet shelter. Local schools may need help in the classroom. If you have had a successful business career, the Small Business Administration has a program called SCORE (www.score.org) which links retired business people to business people who can gain knowledge and experience these retirees have to offer for no charge.

Find your passion and grow from it. If you found your grief and loneliness overwhelming, and yet over time found yourself, become a counselor. There are programs where you can go to school, become certified, and run grief support groups. In fact, community and local colleges are great sources for inexpensive classes to help find and develop your particular interest.

There are many examples of those who have reinvented themselves later in life. It may be going back to school to become a teacher, learn new technologies, or get an advanced degree. The key is to acknowledge that embracing change can be a good thing and be open to new ideas and opportunities.

AREAS TO CONSIDER

1. Do you feel that you have enough social interaction with other people?
   a) If you answered "no," what are the reasons?
   - Transportation
   - Home is Isolated
   - Friends/Family No Longer Live in Area
   - Other/Explain:

2. Do you want more access to entertainment?
   a) If you answered "yes," what kind of entertainment do you prefer?
   - Theatre
   - Dance
   - Music
   - Movies
   - Reading
   - Educational/Personal Development

3. Would you like more information on volunteer opportunities in your community?

4. Do you have enough activity in your life to keep you occupied?

   a) If you answered "no", what are you missing?
- Adult Education
- Exercise
- Entertainment
- Parties and Social Events
- Social Clubs
- Travel
- Other/Explain:

5. What concerns do you have regarding social and community connections?

For more Areas to Consider related to the Social Engagement Pillar, download the *Act III: Your Plan for Aging in Place* at https://naipc.memberclicks.net/ or scan the QR code:

3
Twelve Actions to Prepare for a Safer Future

We asked four of our authors to share their best actions for preparing a safe and engaging future for aging in place. May the following ideas and insights be helpful as you put together your aging in place plan.

C. Vicki Gold, PT, MA:

Maintaining our best health possible as we age, and age in place, is to remain active with exercise and/or movement. For readers who enjoy lists, here is a concise checklist of my best practices to review and apply to your lifestyle.

1. Stay on top of your medical and physical check-ups.

2. Take necessary steps to manage current medical or physical conditions.

3. Learn about the steps you should take to prevent unwanted health conditions.

4. Take advantage of services that will assist you in maintaining better health and safety.

5. Get assessed by a physical therapist. Many of these professionals specialize in areas such as geriatrics, orthopedics, neurology, cardio-pulmonary, etc. Be sure to ask.

6. Visit the American Physical Therapy Association (APTA) website. It is an outstanding resource. The website is: www.apta.org.

7. Do your research and learn more about any conditions you have. Here is a list of some of the common health issues older adults experience:
• Arthritis - www.arthritis.org
• Osteoporosis - www.bonehealthandosteoporosis.org
• Heart Health - www.heart.org
• Lung Disease - www.lung.org

8. There are innumerable resources in libraries and online regarding mind-body, traditional, and functional exercises. Use them, but with special attention to your physical safety and well-being. Remember to include The ABC System (Align, Breathe, Center) shared in the Health & Wellness section in the book as part of any exercise or activity.

9. Include family and friends in your fitness and well-being program. It can help motivate you and may also help them!

10. Keep a positive attitude and stay active.

11. One of my favorite resources for a foot and ankle exercise device - resistancedynamics.com/movemor

12. Another helpful resource for a stepper and body exerciser - www.xiser.com.

Fritzi Gros-Daillon, MS, CSA, CAPS, UDCP, SHSS:

We have all heard the grim warning: falls are the leading cause of death among older adults, beating car accidents and diseases. Here are some facts to consider:

a) One in three adults over age sixty-five will fall each year.
b) One in two adults over the age of eighty will fall each year.
c) Most falls occur inside the home.
d) The likelihood for a repeat fall is two out of three people within a year.

The statistics did not improve during the COVID-19 pandemic years. A University of Michigan 2021 study indicated that the rate of falling increased due to reduced exercise, mobility, and muscle strength, resulting in confinement to home and closure of exercise options and locales.

Get a Home Safety Assessment

Fortunately, falls are a preventable epidemic, but only if we invest the time and resources to minimize them. One of the tools for reducing the risks of falls is the home safety assessment. It is the best place to start to identify the risks in the current home environment, be it lighting, clutter, throw rugs, and more.

Age Safe America offers a certification training program called Senior Home Safety Specialist in the online format, covering a holistic curriculum with seventeen topic modules and a focus on evaluation of the home, exteriors and interior, room-by-room. The information can be found at www.agesafeamerica.com. There are other resources for home safety information such as the National Aging in Place Council, AARP, and Rebuilding Together (www.rebuildingtogether.org). With the right instructive tools, you can certainly make an educated effort to perform your own home assessment. But there's no substitute for the value a trained professional delivers with up-to-date, practical and implementable recommendations-often, immediately and while they are still in your home.

Here are a few examples of important safety tips for the home to reduce the risk of falls.

1. Install grab or safety bars, especially in the bathroom.

Over a quarter million people fall in the bathroom each year. Grab bars can be installed in the tub and shower areas, typically horizontally in the shower. A vertical grab bar can be installed as you step into the tub or shower for support. There are accessories that are designed to meet the support requirements and serve other purposes as well. For example, a soap dish grab bar or shower shelf grab bar can be installed to be just that - simply a soap dish or shower shelf, but it will also be a place to hold onto to steady yourself in the shower. The toilet paper dispenser can be replaced with a toilet paper grab bar as a support for extra assistance getting up and down. There are many more locations and styles of grab bars and safety bars that will integrate into your bathroom design aesthetic.

2. Install handrails and safety bars in the home.

In the broader look at the home, there are other places where handrails or safety bars can be considered. Examples include the steps between the garage and the door to the house, the front or back steps, the walkway out to the trash or recycling bin area, and along hallways and even closets. Many people still hold to the belief that grab bars are ugly, or that they scream "old age." Consider that fashion has entered the home safety industry. Now there are any number of camouflaged and stylish options. And the practical reality is that at some point, it is just the right thing to choose our safety and well-being over all other considerations or concerns.

3. Lighting to ensure rooms and other areas are properly illuminated.

Lighting is another key area in which an assessment of the current situation may provide some easy, practical solutions to make improvements and reduce falls. First, consider solar lights and motion sensor lights to illuminate outside along pathways during dusk, nighttime hours, and even cloudy days.

In the garage, there is typically a garage door opener light and maybe one overhead additional light with a switch. Changing the individual bulb to an LED individual or multi-bulb fixture will enhance the lighting to make the garage to house transition safer. Inside the home, lighting is important, too. As we age, we need more light to conduct the same tasks easily. Changing to LED bulbs can add brightness efficiently. Look at the lighting in specific areas of the home like the hallways and closets. Add night lights to the bathroom and kitchen. Using the new LED tape lights under vanity cabinets, toe-kicks under kitchen cabinets, along stairs or stair railings and hallways, are other great ideas to brighten the home and add safety.

Emergency Preparation

The first step in emergency preparation is to anticipate the emergencies you are likely to encounter. Do you live in an area prone to flooding, hurricanes, wildfires, or earthquakes? The answer will determine the specifics of your emergency kit and supplies. Remember, however, a general emergency kit is always handy and can be purchased or secured through organizations such as the American Red Cross.

Once you understand the emergencies for which you will prepare, the next step is to assess your current situation. Develop your personal contact network; not just the local fire department and emergency service phone numbers, but what are the contact numbers for your list? Do you have work, home, and mobile phone numbers? Your contacts may be affected by the same emergency so multiple means of contacting them is important.

Next, you need to have an emergency escape plan from the house to a designated safe location away from the house. Determine the exits from the rooms in case of a house fire or any other emergency, and identify the safe meeting location. Consider both daytime and nighttime emergency exits, and the path to the meeting spot. The plan should be communicated to all family members and caregivers (family or professional) and practiced.

If you are leaving the property, take the emergency supplies with you, including vital documents and medication. Remember to include supplies for any pets, too. Many organizations provide very detailed checklists for supplies with recommended quantities if the emergency will keep you out of the home for three days or more. Here is a link to the Red Cross list: www.redcross.org/get-help/how-to-prepare-for-emergencies/survival-kit-supplies.html or you can check their website for more general information.

The important part of emergency preparation is actually doing it. My advice is simple: put a date on the calendar and tackle the first step and then schedule the days to complete the task. Every six months, you need to check the supplies, update the medication lists, refresh supplies as needed, and you will be ready.

Personal Emergency Response
For many of us, the key to a safer future begins with a safer today. Each of these suggestions is designed to prompt us to be proactive about our decisions and opportunities today for which our future selves will be grateful. Personal emergency response systems have been available for decades. The one with which we are most familiar is the First Alert system and the famous tagline, "I've fallen and I can't get up." The systems have grown from simple necklace pendants connected via a phone landline, to emergency services, to

fall detection applications in smartphones, and wearable devices as bracelets and watches.

First consider your location and access to emergency services in case of a sudden fall or medical issue. Then determine the best response system - phone, local EMTs and/or family members or caregivers. Evaluate the companies and product choices that best meet your current and future (or anticipated) needs.

The increasing sophistication in the technology has advanced from the simple fall alert system to full telehealth/telemedicine monitoring. It makes the product evaluation more arduous, but you can simplify the search by first understanding your own specifications. This can reduce feeling overwhelmed about all the product's bells and whistles. Certainly, there is a budgetary component as well, but our safety and peace of mind are invaluable.

There are many examples where a personal emergency response system was invaluable. One client, with vertigo and other underlying medical conditions, felt she was falling but staggered to unlock the front door, pressed the alert button and then lost consciousness. Luckily, the EMTs dispatched to her home were able to revive her and transport her to the hospital. She recovered from the incident and returned home, grateful for the alert system. There are also many tragic stories about comparable circumstances with devastating results. It is our choice to make a safer future by informed decisions for our well-being and those of our family members.

Gina Knight:

The best way to educate families, older adults, and the community is sharing my client stories and our relationships with them. These stories best describe our all-inclusive dedication to care and compassion helping older adults transition through the stages of their lives.

People always ask me to share real life scenarios of how I have helped older adults successfully age in place. Let me share one story with you that provide an example of what can be done to create an aging in place plan.

Meet Jean - a sixty-eight-year-old widow living in Burr Ridge, Illinois. Jean has two sons in their fifties. As busy professionals, they hired a professional care manager in Schaumburg, Illinois to assist their mother while they attended multiple medical appointments learning about her unexpected medical condition.

Preparing Jean's Age in Place Plan

In my company, we work with several patient advocates and professional care managers as trusted professional partners. Following a diagnosis of late onset multiple sclerosis, we were contacted by the care manager to begin working with the family on how they were going to deal with this "crisis." Jean's condition was an unexpected health decline. We worked with the family on preparing for the future so Jean could successfully Age in Place. Unfortunately, Jean was eventually going to be on a path of losing the ability to move freely around her home and take care of herself. Jean wished to remain in her home as long as possible.

Our first step was to develop an Age in Place assessment, a plan specifically designed for Jean. The home where Jean lived was a raised ranch, which helped avoid the complexities of a second floor. Once the plan was agreed upon, we worked on making the immediate changes within the home. The following were the changes based on Jean's Age in Place plan:

- Redesigned the bathroom, installing a barrier free roll-in shower with a new comfort height toilet.
- Installed a wall-hung shower seating area along with grab bars and hand-held showerhead for the caregiver to assist Jean. We replaced the existing bathroom door with a pocket door along with greater doorway expansion.
- Replaced existing sink vanity. We installed a wall-hung sink to accommodate wheelchair access. This enabled Jean to roll up to the sink and brush her teeth, apply make-up, and brush her hair. It was very important to help Jean maintain some of her independence.
- Widened all doorways in the home to accommodate wheelchair access.
- Replaced the flooring to adjust the varying heights throughout the home to be the same level. This allowed Jean to move around her home independently without a caregiver.
- Installed a permanent exterior ramp both in front and back of the home. Not only did this provide access in and out for doctor appointments, but it also allowed Jean to continue to enjoy her beautiful yard.
- Relocated the laundry room from basement to first floor.

All the above changes put Jean on the road to a greater level of independence while remaining in her home.

Create Your Age in Place Plan

Part of everyone's Age in Place plan should begin in their fifties by first establishing trusted partners. Having the right attorney for proper legal documentation to establish a will, trust and/or power of attorney (POA) for health and residence along with financial planners, becomes imperative when unexpected circumstances and expenses arise.

We connected Jean to the proper resources within our trusted professional network to enable her to prepare for the rest of her life. If you do not have your Age in Place Plan organized, I encourage you to start today.

Ryan McEniff:

There are three important tips that I can give you to start preparing for a safer future today.

Tip 1: Planning

It is important to have all your affairs in order: your will, healthcare proxy and advance care plan. In the event you cannot speak for yourself, having a trusted person to carry out your wishes is priceless.

We received a call from one of our caregivers who was upset. The client she was caring for was dying, and her family was arguing loudly in the adjacent room. Our client had expressed her wishes, but had not documented them. Her children had different interpretations and memories of what those wishes were. They spent her last hours arguing rather than enjoying moments by her bedside.

Go to Google and search your state and use the keywords "healthcare proxy form" to find your state's specific form. If you change your mind, you can always create a new health care proxy form.

To establish your advance care plan, look at websites like Honoring Choices and Five Wishes (www.fivewishes.org). Their templates provide food for thought and will help you develop your individualized plan.

These two forms will make it much easier for your doctors and family members to carry out your final wishes.

Tip 2: Home Modifications

Making modifications to a home is imperative if an older adult wants to stay in the home indefinitely. As I said earlier in the book, an ounce of prevention is worth a pound of cure.

Install grab bars everywhere that make sense. Reinforce external and internal stair railings so they are weight-bearing (as many internal rails are not). In the kitchen and bathroom, use non-slip pads to prevent falls. Install a raised toilet seat, shower chair, or a low-profile tub will make the bathroom much safer. You can arrange an in-home assessment through a local occupational or physical therapist.

Everything mentioned above will cost less than a few thousand dollars to have done. Compare that to in-home private home care, assisted living, or skilled nursing facilities. You will then see how inexpensive these home modifications can be.

I cannot stress enough how often I see families waiting until after a crisis occurs to install these types of safety features in the home. Eventually, aging adults will need these items, so installing them sooner rather than later is strongly recommended.

A client we had just started caring for declined home modification suggestions as well as continued in-home care services. The adult-children begrudgingly agreed to see how their parent would do on their own before putting their foot down. Unfortunately, the senior fell down a flight of stairs a week after being discharged from the rehab unit and passed away shortly after.

Tip 3: Manage Expectations
Most families who call for services had no idea these services existed the days prior to mom entering the hospital.

Ideally, families will have done some quick research (e.g., reading blogs, watching videos, and talking with other families who have gone through this process) about what to expect. As the agency, that means we need to be clear about what our customers should expect from us.

Understanding what home care provides, the pros and cons of choosing in-home care over other services, will allow you to manage your expectations and lower your stress by knowing an agency is fulfilling this end of the arrangement. If they are not, you will have the knowledge to spot this and can switch to another agency. Every agency is different, so not everything is comparable, but the bulk of it is.

At the very least, be prepared and do some Google searches to see what questions to ask or refer to the checklist "What Questions Should I ask When Interviewing a Caregiver or Home Care Agency" in the Resources section of the Housing pillar. I believe that a reputable agency should have a wealth of information for you to learn from on their website to help you make the right decision.

Let me give you an example. I invite you to listen to my podcast, The Caregiver's Toolbox. It is free. There are no ads, and I make no money from it. It is a labor of love to give information to families who are interested in learning more about senior care topics. You can find it at: https://podcasts.apple.com/us/podcast/the-caregivers-toolbox/id1183027228.

In addition to blogs, videos, and podcasts, there are plenty of books to read or listen to. I recommend you look at the National Aging in Place's resources on their web page. In addition to a blog, you can download the *Act III: Your Plan for Aging in Place* booklet. Also, stop by and listen to the *Aging in Place Conversations with Tara and Ryan* podcast at www.blubrry.com/aginginplace. It features some motivation and stories behind the members of the National Aging in Place Council. Tara Ballman, the Executive Director of the National Aging in Place Council (an author in this book, too), joins me on the program.

Here is my point; the more time you invest in being prepared, the less stress you and your family will have when the time comes to successfully age in place.

4
What Should You Do Next?

Now that you have had the opportunity to read through *Aging in Place Conversations: What Industry Experts Have to Say*, it is time to put your knowledge into action!

To begin, stop by and visit the National Aging in Place Council's website at https://ageinplace.org to search for resources in your area. Download your own free copy of *Act III: Your Plan for Aging in Place* at https://naipc.memberclicks.net or email us at NAIPC@ageinplace.org for an electronic or paper copy. It is a twenty-four-page question-based document that applies our Five Pillars to help you develop your own customized Aging in Place plan. It will guide you through the five main areas that impact your safety, health, and overall well-being to age in place: **Housing, Health and Wellness, Personal Finance, Transportation, and Community and Social Interaction.**

If you wish to receive additional assistance, please contact us at

NAIPC
PO Box 3741
Costa Mesa, CA 92627
Email: NAIPC@ageinplace.org

Start Your Online Assessment:
https://ageinplace.org/myneeds/

We at the National Aging in Place Council, and the contributing authors to this book, hope you have found *Aging in Place Conversations: What Industry Experts Have to Say* to be a valuable resource to begin your journey of successfully aging in place. We strongly believe that each person has the ability to choose the best approach to enjoy and thrive in the life they wish to live. New opportunities and dreams are waiting for you. Start today to prepare for the amazing life ahead as you age in place!

Biographical Index of Contributing Authors

The contributing authors for this book are NAIPC members throughout the United States. Each brings a unique and specialized expertise to the questions presented. Each author welcomes you to contact them if you have specific questions.

Tara Ballman, MBA
Executive Director
National Aging in Place Council
www.ageinplace.org
www.taraballman.com

Tara Ballman currently serves as Executive Director for the National Aging in Place Council, where she brings professionals and communities together to champion aging-in-place through collaboration and education. She has worked in the aging services marketplace since 2003, authored 3 books on reverse mortgages, and co-hosts a NAIPC podcast.

Bonnie Dobbs
Founder/Owner
Medicare and Other Red Tape, LLC
www.medicareandotherredtape.com

Bonnie Dobbs is founder/owner of Medicare and Other Red Tape, LLC, a Medicare insurance broker. She is a leading speaker for workshops/seminars, a trainer, and panelist on the topic of Medicare. Bonnie is the Medicare insurance expert with The Atlanta Journal-Constitution for their Aging in Atlanta series. She is chair of the Greater Atlanta Chapter, NAIPC.

Scott Fulton
President
Home Ideations
www.homeideations.com
www.longevityadvantage.com

Scott Fulton is President, Home Ideations; Chair, National Aging in Place Council's Board of Directors; Longevity and Healthspan Educator, Universities of Virginia and Delaware campuses; Member, American College of Lifestyle Medicine; Engineering graduate, St. Lawrence College. A recognized innovator and thought leader on aging, Scott's evidence-based, systems approach is refreshingly effective and impactful.

Mary Kay Furiasse, BSN, JD, LLM
Founder
A/Z Health & Elder Law
www.azhealthelderlaw.com

Mary Kay Furiasse is founder of A/Z Health & Elder Law, a Life Care Planning law firm focused on elder law. She has over 30 years' experience in practice. She is a Board-Certified Patient Advocate, member of the Legislative Committee for AgeGuide Northeastern Illinois, DuPage County Bar Association, Illinois State Bar Association, American Bar Association Elder & Health Law Sections, and the Life Care Planning Law Firms Association. She is active with the National Aging in Place Council.

Ronnie Genser
President
Bereavement Navigators
www.bereavementnavigators.com

Ronnie Genser works with widows/widowers and adult children on all the tasks they will face after the death of a loved one. She also helps healthy baby boomers create a personal succession plan, similar to a "lifeboat drill," to ensure a smooth transition when one's affairs need to be managed by a loved one or friend.

C. Vicki Gold, PT, MA
Owner, President
Thera-Fitness, Inc.
www.thera-fitness.com

C. Vicki Gold is a retired physical therapist with over 50 years of experience in clinical and academic settings. Her trainings include Yoga, Tai Chi, Pilates, Alexander and Feldendrais Techniques. Vicki is a former Director of the Physical Therapist Assistant Program of LaGuardia Community College, New York. She is the creator of The ABC System and an active public speaker.

Fritzi Gros-Daillon, MS, CSA, CAPS,
UDCP, SHSS
Director, Education and Advocacy,
Age Safe America, LLC
CEO, Household Guardians
https://agesafeamerica.com

Fritzi Gros-Daillon enjoys her encore career as a Master Aging in Place instructor for NAHB and Senior Home Safety Specialist® certification course creator for Age Safe America. A founding member of the NAIPC San Diego chapter, she has served on several nonprofit boards. Her book, Grace and Grit: Insights to Real Life Challenges of Aging, won five national awards. She is a public speaker on aging in place at state and national conferences, radio, and podcasts.

Sue Haviland
CEO and President, Step Smart
www.stepsmart.org

Sue Haviland is a Certified Reverse Mortgage Professional with nearly 20 years' experience in the reverse mortgage industry. She has been an originator, trainer, speaker, and host of the radio show "Senior Spotlight with Sue Haviland" covering senior topics. Sue is president and CEO of Step Smart, a nonprofit educating the public on fall prevention, its risk factors, and actions to make a safer home. She is a Rotary member and serves on NAIPC's National Board of Directors.

Peter Klamkin
Reverse Mortgage Lender
NAIPC National Board Member

Peter Klamkin is director of business development for a top ten reverse mortgage lender, with 17 years' experience in the senior funeral/final expense insurance market before specializing in reverse mortgages for the last sixteen years. He is a board member with National Aging in Place Council, ambassador for the United Network of Organ Sharing, and volunteered with Make A Wish Foundation, Easter Seals, the Muscular Dystrophy Association. He served as chairman of the Life Insurance Council Final Expense Committee.

Gina Knight
Founder and President
Kastle Keeper LLC
www.kastlekeeperllc.com

Gina Knight is founder and president of Kastle Keeper LLC. She has over 30 years' experience in residential/commercial contracting. As an expert in Senior Crisis Management and Aging in Place, she provides professional concierge care offering all-inclusive solutions to seniors and their families. Gina is a Certified Aging in Place Specialist, Illinois Continuity of Care Board Member, and Chairman, National Aging in Place Council - Chicagoland.

Andriana Mendez
Co-Owner
Custom Moving & Hauling
www.custommovehaul.com

Custom Moving & Hauling owners, Art and Andriana, specialize in providing personalized downsizing services. We are Senior Move Manager Certified, and our offerings include sorting, packing, moving, and cleanouts in the San Francisco Bay Area. Our mission, simply put is: Helping you through life's many transitions™.

Amy Miller
Founder, Our Family Encounter
www.ourfamilyencounter.com

Amy Miller is the Founder of Our Family Encounter. No one ages alone. Amy authored Last Life Lesson: A Guide for Seniors and Their Families to meet the needs of the "forgotten middle" older adult who wants to remain in their homes while receiving care from their loved ones.

Ryan McEniff
Owner, Minute Women Home Care
www.mwhomecare.com

Ryan McEniff is the owner of Minute Women Home Care, a family-run business since 1969 located in historic Lexington, MA. He is also the host of the podcast, The Caregiver's Toolbox, which is focused on providing education and information about the senior care industry and Chairs to NAIPC - Massachusetts Chapter.

Wayne Mitchell
Owner, Caring Senior Service
of Northern Virginia
linqapp.com/wayne_mitchell?r=link

Wayne Mitchell is owner of Caring Senior Service of Northern Virginia. As his parents aged and needed assistance, he chose to become a resource for seniors, spouses, and families to navigate the aging process. Wayne is a NAIPC National Board member, Advisory Board member of the Salvation Army, Prince William Corps, and published author.

Courtney Nalty
Founder
Generational Support, LLC
www.generationalsupport.com

Courtney Nalty is the founder of Generational Support, LLC, a caregiver consultancy, and resource guide founded in 2020. Following eleven years with the Continuing Care Retirement Community, in 2017 she began work with a consulting firm that specializes in designing, developing, marketing, and concept ideation for the Active Adult real estate market. Courtney is the author of The Caregiver Toolbox and The Hospital Discharge Handbook.

Deanne O'Rear-Cameron
Mindset Development Specialist
Aging in Place Specialist
www.deanneorear.com
www.ageinplacenevada.org

Deanne is a speaker, author, Mindset Mentor, and Aging in Place Specialist. She empowers people to live their best life through her decade's long experience in Human Development and Aging. She is chair of the City of Las Vegas Senior Citizens Advisory Board, Founder of the Southern Nevada Chapter of the Aging in Place Council, and is on the National Board of NAIPC.

Carmen Perry-Tevaga
Vice President
National Accounts for Veterans Home Care

Carmen Perry-Tevaga is vice president of National Accounts for Veterans Home Care. She has worked in the healthcare industry for nearly twenty years. She specializes in the older adult community. Carmen serves on the VA Council with the Home Care Association of America and is a board member with the NAIPC.

Julianne Rizzo RN, MBA, CSA
Certified Senior Advisor
Oasis Senior Advisor of
Southwest Chicago
https://www.oasissenioradvisors.com
/southwest-chicago/

Julianne Rizzo is a Certified Senior Advisor. She provides free assistance to older adults who want to make their next move to safer living and/or care options. Julianne develops a comprehensive action plan for clients to downsize, transition to senior living, or age in place. She follows all HIPPA compliance regulations to maintain client privacy.

Steve Toll, BS, QDCS
Co-Founder Prescription Music
www.prescriptionmusic.com
www.joyfulmemories.com

Steve Toll co-founded Prescription Music with his wife Linda. As a classically trained musician and composer, he researched and developed a power-of-music philosophy to use music as a therapeutic tool. The company's mission is to educate the public about the power of music. Steve has been a keynote speaker and trainer for the National Alzheimer's Association, agencies, and companies throughout the United States.

Julia Uhll
Senior Real Estate Specialist
Realty ONE Group

Julia Uhll is on a mission to improve the lives of others. She is a Senior Real Estate Specialist with 20 years' experience in real estate. Currently with Realty ONE Group in San Diego, CA, 90 percent of her business is with seniors. Julia serves as an advocate with the local senior and special needs community in San Diego. She and husband Ossie Arciniega are proud parents of their son, AJ, who has Williams Syndrome.

Notes and Additional Resources

In the Notes and Additional Resources chapter, we have provided additional websites, articles, and books to supplement the insights provided by the contributing authors of this book. We encourage you to review these resources to enhance your knowledge about the very important topic of aging in place.

Pillar 1: Housing

Many local resources are available to support older adults maintaining independence in their communities. Scan the QR code to go to the listed website.

1. Eldercare Locator

To find a community program near you, visit the Eldercare Locator and enter your zip code:
https://eldercare.acl.gov/Public/Resources/LearnMoreAbout/Support_Services.aspx

2. National Institute on Aging

https://www.nia.nih.gov/health/aging-place-growing-older-home

3. Single Family Housing Repair Loans & Grants

https://www.rd.usda.gov/programs-services/single-family-housing-programs/single-family-housing-repair-loans-grants

4. The Centers for Disease Control and Prevention (CDC)

The CDC has a website devoted to the topic of Older Adult Fall Prevention, including articles, fall facts, statistics, interventions, resources, and journal articles that provide readers with the knowledge for better and healthier aging. https://www.cdc.gov/falls/index.html.

5. National Association of Home Builders: Aging-in-Place Remodeling Checklist

https://www.nahb.org/education-and-events/education/designations/Certified-Aging-in-Place-Specialist-CAPS/Additional-Resources/Aging-In-Place-Remodeling-Checklist

6. National Adult Day Services Association: How to Choose a Center

https://www.nadsa.org/for-caregivers/choosing-a-center/

7. National Respite Network and Resource Center

https://archrespite.org/consumer-information

8. National Association for Home Care & Hospice: Consumer Resources

https://www.nahc.org/consumers-information/

9. National Association of Senior Move Managers

10. Home Ideation Aging-in-Place Scorecard

Complete a 10-category self-assessment at https://www.homeideations.com/aging-in-place-scorecard/ and your results will be emailed.

11. Can I Get Paid to Care for a Family Member?

https://www.caregiver.org/faq/can-i-get-paid-to-care-for-a-family-member/

12. Family Caregiver Alliance: Hiring In-Home Help

https://www.caregiver.org/resource/hiring-home-help/

13. Michelle R. Davis, "Despite Pandemic, Percentage of Older Adults Who Want to Age in Place Stays Steady," AARP (article), November 18, 2021,

https://www.aarp.org/home-family/your-home/info-2021/home-and-community-preferences-survey.html

14. "What Questions Should I Ask When Interviewing a Caregiver or Home Care Agency" by Wayne Mitchell

15. Rehm, Diane. 2016. On My Own. New York: Alfred A. Knopf.

Pillar 2: Health and Wellness

1. **National Council on Aging's Benefits CheckUp**
Benefits CheckUp connects older adults with benefits programs that can help pay for healthcare, medicine, utilities, and other aging-related services. Search by zip code to find the resources available in your area at https://benefitscheckup.org/

2. Senior Medicare Patrol (SMP)

SMP is a free resource that assists Medicare beneficiaries, their families, and caregivers in preventing, detecting, and reporting healthcare fraud, errors, and abuse. To find assistance in your state or to report potential fraud, visit https://www.smpresource.org/ or scan below:

3. Aging & Disability Networks

The Administration for Community Living (ACL) is comprised of local, state, and national organizations that support older adults. For a list of programs they support, visit https://acl.gov/programs/aging-and-disability-networks or scan below:

4. PhRMA's Medicine Assistance Took

is a search engine designed to help patients, caregivers and healthcare providers match patients with resources and cost-sharing programs that may lower out-of-pocket costs. https://medicineassistancetool.org/

5. National Institute on Aging: Health Topics from A - Z

https://www.nia.nih.gov/health/topics

Pillar 3: Personal Finance

1. The Certified Financial Planner Board offers a guide called Questions To Ask When Choosing A Financial Planner. Get your copy by visiting

https://www.letsmakeaplan.org/how-to-choose-a-planner/10-questions-to-ask-your-financial-advisor.

2. Find a Certified Financial Planner at

https://www.letsmakeaplan.org/

3. Elder Abuse Resources: National Center on Elder Abuse

Education & Awareness materials may be found at
https://ncea.acl.gov/What-We-Do/Education.aspx

4. Money Smart for Older Adults Program, Federal Deposit Insurance Corporation

https://www.fdic.gov/resources/consumers/money-smart/teach-money-smart/money-smart-for-older-adults.html

5. Veteran Service Offices helps write and submit claims to the VA. Find your local office at:

https://nvf.org/veteran-service-officers/

6. VA Aid & Attendance information

https://www.va.gov/pension/aid-attendance-housebound/

7. American Association of Daily Money Managers

https://secure.aadmm.com/

8. U.S. Securities & Exchange Commission

https://www.investor.gov/additional-resources/information/seniors

9. Financial Literacy & Education Commission

https://www.mymoney.gov/lifeevents

10. Social Security Retirement Planner

https://www.ssa.gov/benefits/retirement/

11. Veterans Administration

https://www.va.gov/

12. If you would like to use your VA Aid and Attendance funds primarily for home care or adult day care and receive care before a VA check arrives, contact the Veterans Home Care regarding their VetAssist Program at 888-314-6075 or visit www.veteranshomecare.com

13. The Federal Interagency Forum on Aging-Related Statistics brings together aging-related data from Federal agencies.

https://agingstats.gov/about.html

Pillar 4: Transportation

1. Mordor Intelligence
https://www.mordorintelligence.com/industry-reports/ridesharing-market#

2. National Aging in Place Council's Act III: Your Plan for Aging in Place is an excellent resource to begin conversations related to transportation. This is a free download on naipc.memberclicks.net.

3. Researchers at the University of Missouri-St. Louis (UMSL) have created a checklist that considers emotional and attitudinal awareness, not just logistics. This is an excellent document to initiate thoughts about future transportation needs. Don't let its very technical title - "Assessment of Readiness for Mobility Transition" (ARMT) - scare you. This one-page checklist and directions can be found at:
https://www.umsl.edu/mtci/PDFs/ARMT_2011c.pdf

4. **The American Occupational Therapy Association is another excellent resource. It provides a Driving & Community Mobility Toolbox and supports the CarFit workshops, which analyzes if the vehicle is appropriate for the driver.**

For more information, visit www.aota.org/olderdriver and www.car-fit.org.

5. **The Clearinghouse for Older Road User Safety is supported by the Department of Transportation and the National Highway Traffic Safety Administration.**

They have a library of resources available to older adults, families, medical professionals, and law enforcement and can provide specific state guidance. For more information, visit www.roadsafeseniors.org.

6. Family Conversations with Older Drivers

Resources and online seminars provided by The Hartford
Center for Mature Market Excellence and the MIT AgeLab
https://www.thehartford.com/resources/mature-market-
excellence/family-conversations-with-older-drivers

7. Easterseals Transportation Options for Seniors and Caregivers

https://www.easterseals.com/support-and-education/for-
caregivers/transportation-for-seniors.html

Pillar 5: Community and Social Interaction

1. Volunteers in Action

https://voa.org

2. AARP

https://www.aarp.org/volunteer/virtual/

3. SCORE

https://score.org/

4. Author Amy Miller hosts a free weekly online video conference meeting for anyone to join on Monday mornings at 9:00 a.m. (Central Time).

Here is the link for more information:
https://bluejeans.com/894862251/2337

5. Elderhostel: Learning Adventures Across the Globe
https://www.roadscholar.org/

6. The Oasis Institute
Promotes healthy aging through lifelong learning, active lifestyles, and volunteer engagement.
https://www.oasisnet.org/

7. American Horticultural Therapy Association
https://www.ahta.org/

8. American Music Therapy Association
https://www.musictherapy.org/

9. AARP's Experience Corps Volunteer Program
https://www.aarp.org/experience-corps/

10. Little Brothers: Friends of the Elderly
https://lbfenetwork.org/

11. AmeriCorp Seniors

https://americorps.gov/serve/americorps-seniors

The Five Pillars Questions Index

Below is a quick-reference of the main questions that are addressed in this book for each of the Five Pillars. The page number provided is where the question is listed with responses to follow by the applicable contributing author.

Pillar 1: Housing

Question 1: I hear different opinions on housing as people age. It makes it very confusing. Some recommend moving to an assisted living community while others are moving to be closer to their families. I would like to remain in my home, but I need to understand my options. (10)

Question 2: My spouse is coming home from the hospital and prefers to heal comfortably at home. He will be in a wheelchair for a few months, maybe longer. Our home is not wheelchair accessible. Can he stay at home? Who do I call to get help? Can any services be provided in at home to help me? What home modifications do I need? (22)

Question 3: I live alone and have no children. I enjoy my home and keep busy with my interests. Is it okay for me to stay in my home? Are there things I should do to better manage aging in place? (37)

Pillar 2: Health and Wellness

Question 1: I live on my own and can take care of myself. My children don't accept that I can manage things on my own at home. What can I do to make them feel comfortable with me remaining at home on my own? (42)

Question 2: A main concern of individuals aging in place is falling. How can I create greater safety at home? Is decluttering my home an important first step to avoiding falls? What does this involve? What if I need help? (52)

Question 3: I was recently diagnosed with a disease. How do I tell my family? How do I prepare personally? (61)

Question 4: What can I do to develop better balance and physical conditioning so I can stay safe and independent at home? (64)

Pillar 3: Personal Finance

Question 1: What costs do I need to consider, and what income sources are available whether I move to a community or remain in my home? (72)

Question 2: How do I choose a trustworthy financial planner? (75)

Question 3: Mom and Dad have financial investments in different accounts and banks. As the grown children, we are concerned they are not closely tracking their finances. How can we access their accounts, if needed? What is the best way to begin? (76)

Question 4: How do I protect myself from financial fraud or abuse? (77)

Question 5: I have a blended family. What is the best approach to keep peace in the family when it comes to my finances? If I wish to provide for everyone, how should I go about it? (78)

Question 6: What is the difference between capacity and competency? Why do I need a Power of Attorney (POA) to protect myself? (80)

Question 7: What Is Medicare Part A, B, C, and D? (81)

Question 8: When do I sign up to start Medicare? (82)

Question 9: Medicare can get a little complicated. Am I required to sign up for Medicare even if I have medical coverage with my current employer? (83)

Question 10: What are the penalties, if any, if I don't sign up for Medicare? (84)

Pillar 4: Transportation

Question 1: I worry about transportation to go to the doctor or the store. My family is not always available, and I'm afraid to use a ride-sharing service. What are my alternatives for transportation? (109)

Question 2: What is the best way to approach a loved one when it is time for them to stop driving? (117)

Pillar 5: Community and Social Interaction

Question 1: When I grew up, the retirement age was 65. However, I don't see myself retiring any time soon because I'm still able and want to work. Has this expectation in society changed? (123)

Question 2: I have remained updated about technology. How much do I need to know to manage my personal and work life? (126)

Question 3: I work with young people and want to be a better communicator with them. How do I stay relevant so I don't sound like an "old" person? (131)

Question 4: How do I stay socially connected to the people in my life circle, i.e., family, friends, community, doctors, or house of worship? (133)

Question 5: I recently lost my spouse. It seems like all my friends are passing away. I'm feeling lonelier than ever before in my life. What is the best way to deal with bereavement? (137)

~ ~ ~

START YOUR PLAN TODAY

Complete the form below to receive a copy of NAIPC's Act III planning template.

If you have questions about your aging in place plan and would like assistance, please also include your phone or email below.

PLEASE SEND MORE INFOMATION TO:

Name

Address

Address2

City, State, Zip

Phone

Email

I need help with:

SEND TO

✉ NAIPC@ageinplace.org

📍 PO Box 3741, Costa Mesa, CA 92627

OR SCAN TO DOWNLOAD

START YOUR PLAN TODAY

Complete the form below to receive a copy of NAIPC's Act III planning template.

If you have questions about your aging in place plan and would like assistance, please also include your phone or email below.

PLEASE SEND MORE INFOMATION TO:

Name

Address

Address2

City, State, Zip

Phone

Email

I need help with:

SEND TO

✉ NAIPC@ageinplace.org

📍 PO Box 3741, Costa Mesa, CA 92627

OR SCAN TO DOWNLOAD

START YOUR PLAN TODAY

Complete the form below to receive a copy of NAIPC's Act III planning template.

If you have questions about your aging in place plan and would like assistance, please also include your phone or email below.

PLEASE SEND MORE INFOMATION TO:

Name

Address

Address2

City, State, Zip

Phone

Email

I need help with:

SEND TO

✉ NAIPC@ageinplace.org

📍 PO Box 3741, Costa Mesa, CA 92627

OR SCAN TO DOWNLOAD